Walking

IN THE

FOG

By Barbara Steger

Walking in the FOG

Trilogy Christian Publishers A Wholly Owned Subsidary of Trinity Broadcasting Network
2442 Michelle Drive Tustin, CA 92780

Trilogy Christian Publishing/TBN and colophon are trademarks of Trinity Broadcasting Network. For information about special discounts for bulk purchases, please contact Trilogy Christian Publishing.

Trilogy Disclaimer: The views and content expressed in this book are those of the author and may not necessarily reflect the views and doctrine of Trilogy Christian Publishing or the Trinity Broadcasting Network.

Manufactured in the United States of America

10 9 8 7 6 5 4 3 2 1
Library of Congress Cataloging-in-Publication Data is available.

ISBN: 978-1-64773-737-5
E-ISBN: 978-1-64773-738-2

DEDICATION

I dedicate this book to the love of my life, Fredrick Andre Steger—affectionately called Daddy-Fred, and the man I have been married to for over half of my lifetime. You have been my rock, my protector, my shoulder to cry on, my lover, and my best friend. Thank you for always supporting my hopes and dreams. I am so glad I get to do life with you. And if I had to do it all over again, I would still accept that ride in your little baby blue '76 Fiat Spider. Who knew that ride would turn into all of this??!!

ACKNOWLEDGEMENTS

I want to thank my Lord and Savior, Jesus Christ. Because He stepped in as my substitute, I have a right to the tree of life. Because of Him, I am free. His love towards me is unwavering and causes me to want to know Him more and more. Thank you, Jesus!

A very sincere and loving "thank you" goes to my parents, Bishop Qullias and Pastor Denise Mitchell. You both taught me how to be strong and how to stand firm on the promises of faith—to just trust God in spite of what my natural eyes could see or what my natural ears could hear. Thanks for being godly parents and for teaching me right from wrong, even when I did not always want to hear it. I would not be who I am today without your love and guidance. You are revered and honored!

Additionally, I want to thank my dear friend and sister in Christ, Oveta Carey, for writing a foreword for my book. You did not hesitate when I asked, and for that, I am grateful. Thank you for being a godly woman and an example for me to emulate.

I would be remiss if I did not acknowledge my children (as well as to include their spouses and significant others). To Fred (Jeanette and my three grandbabies), Joshua (Chelsea and my three grandbabies), Amber (and my grandson), and Andre´ (Gabriela and my granddaughter). I love you all. You have enriched my life and bring me so much joy! I am honored to be your mother, mother-in-law, and grandma.

And last but not least, I want to say "thank you" to the countless people who will read *Walking in the FOG* and allow it to help mend those broken places in your lives. I wrote this book for you and myself, to show us that no matter how thick the fog is in our lives, we can see clearly because the God of the universe walks with us and He illuminates our path. We are walking in the Favor of God!

TABLE OF CONTENTS

FOREWORD

It is no surprise to me that Barbara Steger has written a book that is insightful, significant, and thought-provoking. Upon meeting her many years ago, she reminded me of the kind of girl I grew up with. Yet there is a uniqueness about her that embraces a quiet confidence to not only survive, but thrive.

Sometimes people operate from the presupposition that those who are happy, well-adjusted, and mature have been that way for a long time. *Walking in the FOG* reminds us that painted smiles are often the impetus for declaring victory despite vulnerabilities. Barbara intricately offers the story behind the story. Hardly missing a stride, she captures the essence of the human spirit. Her forthright style draws us in to life as it is.

She chooses to bring her life experiences that are without exception open, honest, and reflective. Through struggles, illnesses, and triumphs, she is a woman who has done the work. She gives to us what she has given to herself – the freedom to be!

I am extremely proud of Barbara for her heart for God. She follows it with zest and allows each day to fuel it for the next. This book is a poignant reminder of the power of our inner thoughts. When you finish reading *Walking in the FOG*, you will be uplifted by her transformative entries. What a joy it is to watch God shape her life and give her great influence.

—Oveta Carey
Minister and Retired Administrator
Enterprise, AL

FOREWORD

Walking in the FOG is a must read for anyone who acknowledges that sometimes life hurts, and that it is not always fair. This book is for those who can appreciate the fact that the struggle is real and that we are not living in a "spiritual fantasy land" where all our problems just mystically disappear.

Walking in the FOG is birthed from real life experiences. I know because I have known and watched the author for almost fifty years. She has gone from having no relationship with God at all to walking in His favor. I know it has not always been easy, but I also know it has been worth it. Like many others I came to realize that God's favor is not something that can be earned but received and accepted simply by faith.

I am proud of you, "Baby Girl."

—Love, Daddy
Bishop Qullias Mitchell Jr.
Pastor, Phillips Temple AOH Church of God
Pensacola, FL

PREFACE

As I envision the people who will read this book, I see a kaleido-scope of colors, ages, and personalities. I see men and women from all backgrounds and social status—from the haves to the have-nots and everything in between. I see people full of promise and vitality who are searching, reasoning, and questioning both the meaning of life and their roles in this big world. I see groups of people who are united in their quest to gain knowledge, wisdom, and instructions on how to better themselves and the people around them. I commend you for being a seeker of knowledge and for knowing you cannot do it by yourself—you need God to open the ears of your understanding.

Let me start by saying God has a plan for each and every one of our lives, and you are placed on this earth to fulfill a specific purpose and plan. You have a destiny—a predetermined course of events God has destined you for. Jeremiah 29:11 (NIV) says, "For I know the plans I have for you, declares the Lord, plans to prosper you and not harm you, plans to give you a hope and a future." Let's be very clear about something: God makes no mistakes. This means no matter the events surrounding your conception, YOU ARE HERE BY GOD'S DESIGN.

The Master Architect, God, knew you from the very start. In fact, He knew you before you were formed in your mother's womb. That means before you were even conceived by your parents, God had already fashioned you. He knew what you would look like, what you would experience, and who you would become. He already knew YOU!

And now that we know how God sees us, let's talk about how you see yourself. How we see ourselves is critical in our development as people, and especially as believers. How we view ourselves can help us or hinder us in this journey called life. Often times, because of our life experiences, we view ourselves through misconceived and misconstrued information—what I like to refer to as dirty lenses. These dirty lenses exist because of what we have allowed to take root in our hearts and minds about ourselves. Dirty lenses come in the form of what other people have said to us about us. The lenses manifest in what people have done negatively to us, and in some cases, what they should have done but chose not to. Can you say, "Disappointments?" The dirty lenses reappear often in what we say about ourselves. They also show up in the guilt and shame of the wrong things we have done, as well as in the negative and harmful things we have experienced. Can you say, "Self-doubt?" These dirty lenses exist because we have not learned to let go, and the ensuing result is we continue to look through dirty lenses that do not allow us to see things for what they really are. And they don't allow us to see ourselves through the eyes of a loving heavenly Father.

In my many roles of wife, mom, teacher, and minister, I have come across many people much like you and me who are full of promise but view themselves through dirty lenses. They see themselves through the dirty lenses of society and the issues they have faced. In my case, as a person of color, I have seen and experienced firsthand what our society says about children of color. The images I saw and heard told me that I was too black, poor, uneducated, un-teachable, un-coachable, and without hope. Those images said that I lived in the wrong neighborhood, and that I was not smart enough. And those images hurt, not necessarily because they were true, but because I bought into them. You see, we often see ourselves through the hurts and pains of our past. The molestation and rape we experienced as a little child, as well as the physical and mental abuse we have suffered, have hurt us deeply. The abandonment by a parent or the divorce of our parents, which made us the products of broken homes, seemed to be more than we could bare. Or maybe you don't know your parent, leaving you with a perpetual void in your heart. Each of these experiences leaves you longing for more—a longing for purpose and a longing for an identity. And sadly, we often define our worth through the rejection of others. We are too fat, skinny, short, tall, or we just we don't fit in—the list goes on. Essentially, what everyone is saying is that they want you to be ANYBODY but you. Don't fall prey to this trap! You have to learn to reject the negative actions and mindsets of other people and focus on the fact that God fashioned you the way you are for a reason. God, in His infinite wisdom, makes no mistakes. You were purposed by His design!

The real truth to all of this is that many of you are what I consider the "walking wounded." You walk around with a painted smile on your face, acting as if nothing is wrong. You protect yourself by erecting walls to keep people out and to keep them from hurting you again. The sad part about all of this is you really want to be free, and you want to let go. The even sadder part is you don't know how.

And that, my brothers and sisters, was my truth. I suffered in silence, not knowing I could use my voice to activate change in my life. And take notice I wrote, "was," because that is not who or what I am anymore. God came in and broke the shackles off my feet, and for the first time in my life, I felt a freedom I had never experienced before.

This is why I wrote my book, *Walking in the FOG*. I wrote it to help people like you and me who have struggled and continue to struggle with their identity and purpose. I wrote this book so you too could experience the freedom from your past. My prayer is that you will learn who you are and whose you are, allowing you to live a life full of purpose—one that is full of joy and peace, as well as pregnant with God's unmerited grace and favor. I encourage you to take a leap of faith and boldly declare you will not live in your past, and you will forgive those who have hurt and abused you. In doing so, you will commit to making yourself better by strengthening your walk with Christ—because without Him, we cannot do anything of ourselves.

How you live out your life is going to come down to what YOU say and agree about yourself. You must learn to overcome a negative thought with a POSITIVE word. Yes, you have got to OPEN your mouth and speak life to those broken places in your soul Many of you may have read my bio, and you may be thinking to yourselves, "There is no way she has problems or that she can even relate to me." I beg to differ. My life hasn't always been a bed of roses, and I have struggled with understanding my purpose. But I thank God for Jesus, because after I realized God had a purpose and a plan for my life, I began to look at my situation and myself differently. I began to trust what God had to say about me and began to reject the seeds of self-doubt, hate, and rejection. I allowed God to minister to my heart and heal those broken places. I began to encourage myself and to speak life to the many different situations I was experiencing. I won't say to you that life is easy or you will never experience pain and disappointment ever again. However, what I will say is that with God, life is better and full of hope. As He began to change my heart, I began to see through clear lenses. They were no longer dirty, and they did not distort or misconstrue my view. Essentially, what I want you to take from the pages of this book is you can fulfill your hopes and dreams despite the hurts from your past. You can walk in your destiny in spite of what others say you can't do, all because God says you can, and you choose to believe Him at His word.

As you begin to read, you will find that some themes within the book are repetitive. This means you really need to grasp a hold of it because it is important to your spiritual well-being, and these are areas the enemy tends to attack the most. As people of God, it is important for us to understand the enemy's schemes and devices. Our obedience to God, a consistent prayer life, and our praise will thwart the devil's plans.

Remember: The fact you are still here is an indication God isn't through with you yet. Your DESTINY awaits! Let's read to learn how to become people who are Walking in the Favor of God!

—Barbara Steger
Enterprise, Al
July 31, 2020

CHAPTER 1

He Knows Your Name

How precious also are thy thoughts unto me, O God!
how great is the sum of them. If I should count them,
they are more in number than the sand.

—Psalm 139:17-18, KJV

I have often wondered who I would be if I had not experienced some of the pain I have gone through over the course of my life. Instead of being a loner, would I have been the social butterfly whom everyone seemed to be drawn to? Would I have done something so great with my life that the president and Oprah Winfrey would have wanted to share my story and recognize me for my accomplishments? Would I have still married a small-town boy instead of jet-setting across the world? The funny thing is there really is no answer to these hypothetical questions. You see, that is the thing with reflectors, we tend to look back a lot and analyze everything. Reflecting over the way that you handle things is not necessarily a bad thing. Being reflective helps you to find out how to do things differently and how to do them better. In some cases, your motive behind the action is revealed during the reflection process. However, we cannot be so caught up in the reflecting that we cease to live, love, grow, mourn, and move on from the things of our past. Often our lives lack clarity and purpose because we cannot see or feel beyond what we see and feel right now, causing our lives to become stagnant, unfulfilling, and without purpose.

And so it is with the cycle of our lives. The rise and fall of the things we experience act as weights, and they begin to pull us down, just like how the tide of the sea is caused by the moon's gravitational pull on the earth. Our highs and lows become cyclical in nature, and we seem to always to be at the mercy of some new experience, emotion, or even relationship. What we need is a "grounding" that will cause us to live lives full of power, purpose, and prayer. Lives that show others we are walking in the favor of God.

I wrote this book not because I want to show everyone how awesome I am as a person, but to show others how we all share many of the same hurts, disappointments, traumas, losses, setbacks, failures, frustrations, and even joys. I want you to know that I understand exactly where you are. I have often felt the angst of what I consider "wasted years." Those were the years of me walking aimlessly in life without a compass—no real direction, no real purpose, and no real guide. Life just happened all around me, and I did not feel truly alive; I was just going through the motions. I wanted to do stuff, write stuff, say stuff, and be somebody, but I did not know how. You see, pain has a way of robbing you of your joy, and if left unchecked, it has a way of enabling you because pain breeds fear.

I was fearful of everything, although other people never knew it. Quite convincingly, I was really good at hiding my feelings, and over time, I pretended so well that I thought the mask I was wearing was the real me. I had forgotten the core of my identity and did not know who I was anymore. And then, one day, I got tired of wearing the mask, but I still didn't know who I was. For me, that was a very scary place to be. I feared the unknown me, the me who I didn't reveal to the world and, more often than not, the me I didn't reveal to myself. I had so many questions like, "Would I like her? Would others like her? Was she a dreamer? What were her dreams and desires? What did hope look like to her? Does she ever truly find herself? Does she ever learn to love herself? Like herself?" And more important than any of those other questions was, "Does she ever find peace?"

If you would just take a moment to be really transparent, you would see that I am you and you are me. It matters not what you have or do not have in your bank account, your skin's hue, or even

Barbara Steger

who you know. We are all the same. This book is not just about my life and mine alone; it is about all of our lives. It is about the countless lives that are navigating this journey called life. You are treading water but feeling like if things do not change soon, you are not going to make it. It's as if the gravitational pull of the moon on the tide of your very existence is going to pull you under and drown you in your own despair. So I say to you, before you stop treading water, let me help you by navigating this journey not with desperation, fear, and anxiety as we have in times past, but with courage, hope, love, joy, and peace. And I promise if you do, you will see you are not alone, and we are more alike than we are different. Your race, gender, and socio-economic status is not a barrier to our likeness. The biggest, most important thing you and I have in common is the fact that we have a soul that needs saving, and the answer to what ails us lies in our ability to find peace—His name is Jesus. I see you, and I have been there before, but more importantly, God sees you, knows who you are, and He LOVES you immeasurably. He knows your name. Trust me, your life has meaning and purpose; God has been thinking about you since before you were formed in your mother's womb.

The dichotomy that exists in the title of my book, *Walking in the FOG*, deals with how we perceive the issues of our lives. We can choose to believe our journey in life and all its vicissitudes is just a walk in which we know not the path and cannot see our way. Or we can say and believe that we are walking in the favor of God, and that even with all of our struggles, frailties, and mistakes, God is illuminating our path. He walks with us each and every day. He is the light that guides, and we are to trust the process and the path. Will you walk this path of self-discovery through faith with me? Watch how GOD makes you aware of who you are, where you are, and whose you are as you read this book. And when you walk along the path that He has illuminated for you, know that you are Walking in the Favor of God.

LET'S GO!

CHAPTER 2

It's Okay to Cry

...weeping may endure for a night, but joy cometh in the morning.

—Psalm 30:5, KJV

One of the biggest fallacies ever told is the one that says crying is a sign of weakness. In an effort to make our boys and young men tough, our society tells them, "Men don't cry." But if that were the case, why would the Bible tell us, "Jesus wept" (John 11:35, KJV)? And if you know the story of Jesus, you know He endured such hardship in order to ensure our sins were forgiven by God the Father. Surely, with knowing everything He endured to make sure that we had a chance for the tree of life, we would never think Him to be weak. Our tears are often the release of the sadness that pervades our souls. When our souls cannot hold in the pain, they release tiny droplets of water from our eyes that we call tears. Water is such a wonderful thing in that it cleanses, refreshes, and purifies us. Our tears act as the catalyst for release from our pains. In order to weather the storms of life, we must realize that we may have to cry sometimes, but on the other side of those tears and pains is joy if we allow ourselves to truly experience the cleansing nature of water. As we process our pains (and for a great bit of us, there have been many), we cannot forget that often our pains lie in wait for us, waiting to recreate those hurtful moments.

Often, when you think you are over something and really feel as if you have conquered it and shown it the front door, it comes back knocking with a vengeance. That is because it really did not leave.

You showed it the door, but you did not make sure that it and all of its baggage left at the same time. You did not evict it, root and all. The pain found a vulnerable place in your heart and masqueraded behind some other issue in your life. It mimicked its distress call and its mannerisms, hoping you would not find out. And just like a wayward child, even the pain cannot control itself. It wants to be seen and heard, and so the ensuing result is that it betrays itself. As soon as some other bad thing happens to you or enters your life to cause overwhelming discomfort, that old wound rears its ugly head and re-invents itself like a viral mutation fiercely fighting for the dominance and control it once had in your life. Yeah, I know. Pain SUCKS! And yes, I get it. You thought it was gone. You thought you were over the bitter divorce, the molestation you endured as a child, the rape you experienced as a teenager, and the abandonment you felt at the loss of a loved one, whether by death or by choice.

Yeah, I know it hurts to even think about it, yet alone talk about it. Nevertheless, we must be willing to talk about it so that we can begin to mourn, cry, and put those past hurts to death. We MUST have a good cry. You know, the one where your eyes are so swollen from the tears, you have no tears left, and you look like a chipmunk. The one where your nose is snotting for a day, and the release of your tears makes you feel as though you have run a marathon. Yep! That is the one. I feel you, and yes, I have been there too! I get it. Talking about it often feels as though someone has ripped a Band-Aid off a fresh wound with no thought for your feelings. *Sighs*

I know how you feel because that was once my life. I have been there too. So, cry if you must, then cry some more and make sure that you get it all out of your system this time. Why? Because I am giving you one night to cry about it (remember, weeping may endure for a night—that means ONE!), and you can even baby that situation if you want to. However, WE have a place to get to. The new place won't let us take old stuff with us. Joy is waiting, and it refuses to coexist with the pains of your past.

Remember, when your heart is heavy, the best place for you to be is in a place of worship. There is a song, "The Only One" by Antonio Neal, whose verse says, "I cannot move, cannot breathe unless you exhale in me." The phrase "waiting to exhale," made popular by the movie of the same name, centered itself around the search for the perfect mate that, once love was found, would make you exhale. You could breathe again, you could love again, and you could live again. May I suggest the same rings true for you in Christ Jesus? You cannot live, move, or have your being unless you find the love for the Lord of your life. Not only does He cause you to breathe again, but in Him you are a new creature. In Him, you are whole again! Because of Jesus, you can live! Living in Christ is different from living in this world with no hope and no peace. As we surrender to Christ our hopes and even our dreams, the Spirit of Truth will come in and do a work on the inside of you. The Bibles teaches us:

> But when He, the Spirit of Truth, comes, He will guide you into all truth [full of complete truth]. For He will not speak on His own initiative, but He will speak whatever He hears [from the Father—the message regarding the Son], and will disclose to you what is to come [in the future]. He will glorify and honor Me, because He (the Holy Spirit) will take from what is Mine and will disclose it to you. All things that the Father has are Mine. Because of this I said that He [the Spirit] will take from what is Mine and reveal it to you.
>
> —John 16:13-15, AMP

The path will be laid and illuminated so you can begin to walk in your God-given authority. Our lives before Christ were chaotic, full of fear, and without hope. Our lives after coming into agreement with Christ's redemptive work on the cross are explosions of possibilities. With God, all things are possible. Do not settle for less than what God says you can have or what He says you can do. So, cry if you must, and then cry some more. Get it all out, and let your tears be a reminder that water is a refresher and a cleanser. Let your tears be the catalyst to brighter days and restful nights. And now that you have cried it all out, it is time to begin the work so that you can walk in the favor of God.

CHAPTER 3
From Pain to Purpose

And he said unto me, My grace is sufficient for thee: for my strength is made perfect in weakness. Most gladly therefore will I rather glory in my infirmities, that the power of Christ will rest upon me. Therefore I take pleasure in infirmities, in reproaches, in necessities, in persecutions, in distresses for Christ's sake: for when I am weak, then am I strong.

—2 Corinthians 12: 9-10, KJV

As a child, and even to this day, I have always liked to read and hear the Old Testament Bible stories. One of my favorites was Joseph and his coat of many colors. This story outlines the betrayal of Joseph by his brothers as they sell him into slavery and tell his father, Jacob, that some wild animal killed him. It chronicles his journey from his homeland to the pit, the prison, and eventually to the palace, a place he was predestined to go and one that carried a necessity so that he might preserve the generations of Israelites. His decision to honor God and not bemoan his state allowed him to go from the bottom to the top, from the back to the front, from the pit to the palace, from rejected to respected.

The lesson that we can all learn from Joseph is that as long as we live, we will go through some things. We will be mistreated and betrayed often by people who are supposed to be family—those individuals we trust and love, and who are supposed to protect us from hurt, harm, and danger. These people are our mothers, fathers, sisters, brothers, pastors, and/or best friends. The close relationship we have with them is the reason why the betrayal and the sting of their rejection hurts so bad. As bad as it is to have to face what has been done to us, when we face difficulty, we have a decision to make. How are we going to handle the situation? Are we going to be depressed and give up? Are we going to retreat and shut everyone else out of our lives? Are we going to refuse to eat or bathe? (Yes, I have done that too!) You see, these are things that we all have done at some point in our lives after encountering a difficult situation or person. When we gave into our emotions and became emotional, we gave the situation power and control. We can fail to see the things we go through are often necessary to make us into the person we were created and destined to be.

I have often wondered what thoughts Joseph must have had as he was being sold into slavery by his brothers. I wondered how he must have felt when he was accused of trying to have an illicit affair with the king's wife, even though it was not true. I can only imagine the desperation, depression, and dissatisfaction he experienced after helping someone in prison and not having the promise made to him honored. We have people we have helped along in this journey of life, only for them to make it and forget about the help we provided to them. How did that make you feel? If we are to be totally transparent and honest, we would say that we felt bitter. Yes, bitter, angry, and possibly even jealous. We have said things like, "They wouldn't even be in that position if it wasn't for me!" So then, the question that has to be asked is, "Where do we go from there?" Are we going to be bitter or are we going to be better? Are we going to be happy or are we going to be sad? Life is all about choices, and we have a choice to make. Are you going to throw in the towel and give up, or are you going to shake the dew of their rejection off and push forward? Again, we ALL have a choice to make. We can let the situation win and wreak havoc on our emotions, or we can decide to overcome our emotions and be better.

I know it may be hard to see the necessity in many of our situations, but in order for you to grow and heal, we must come to a place in our minds that says, "It happened and it hurt, but I am committed to my healing, and I am committed to being made whole." Commitment, as defined by Webster's Dictionary, means "the state or quality of being dedicated to a cause or activity."[1] Essentially, you must pledge allegiance and alliance to yourself to protect your heart, mind, and emotions. You have to learn to be faithful to yourself and not allow outside stimulation to cause you to become disheartened, disenfranchised, and disillusioned by your God-given purpose. You must press on in spite of what you see and feel, and you should run towards the prize that God has in store for you. You are about to go from the pit to the palace!

Remember, Joseph had a dream. However, he endured many hardships prior to the dream manifesting in his life. He experienced being put in a hole, sold to strangers, alienated from his family, lied on, and put into prison for something he didn't do. Even after he helped someone with their problem, that person forgot to honor the promise of speaking to the king on his behalf. It was not until many years later, after the initial dream, that what God showed him became what he would live. Do not get so focused on the dream that you do not fortify your inner man for the tests, trials, and tribulations that will surely come. Stay the course! Stay focused! Trust God! Your dream will surely come to pass! You will be greater than your former self. The funny thing is that you are not going to be able to recognize yourself because where you are going in the next season of your life will require you to change positions and your name. Think about this: isn't it funny how God always speaks to us as our future selves, but Man keeps speaking to us from who we used to be? The Bible teaches us, "Therefore if any man be in Christ, he is a new creature: old things are passed away; behold, all things are become new" (2 Corinthians 5:17, KJV).

Remember: My brothers and sisters in Christ, we are a NEW creation. We have to stop answering to our old name! Your purpose is waiting, and it no longer knows the old you!

CHAPTER 4

There Is Purpose in Your Afflictions

To everything there is a season, and a time to every purpose under the heaven.

—Ecclesiastes 3:1, KJV

I came across a saying that has stuck with me ever since the first day I read it, and it says, "God loves you too much to waste your pain." Unfortunately, I do not remember who wrote it or where it originated. However, the important thing is that the phrase has resonated deep within me and has caused me to look at my struggles differently. If you are anything like me, your struggles and misfortunes may have caused you to have a distorted view of yourself and, quite honestly, your future. We have to learn to be reflective in our seasons of turmoil. When we allow ourselves to take another look, we are actually giving ourselves a chance to grow. Reflection is defined as giving something "serious thought or consideration."[ii] In order to move forward and not make the same mistakes twice, reflecting must be a part of what we do on a consistent basis. If we want to be better today than we were on yesterday, we must be willing to revisit the decisions we made, as well as the thought processes and emotional states behind them.

The reflective process, when done openly and honestly, should help you to identify the faulty thinking whose roots are grounded in emotional triggers. When you can identify emotional triggers, you can determine what is at the cause of your misconceptions, fears, indecisiveness, anger, bitterness, addictions, hate, promiscuity, and overall godlessness. Being able to identify what is at the root of these things will allow you to not only PRAY your way through, but to allow the Word of God to saturate your heart and settle those things that have been causing you mental and emotional distress. You see, although praying is needful, it is not enough. You must pray and seek the Holy Scriptures because in them are the keys to your deliverance. They are the keys to making your family relationships functional again, to loving yourself, and to finding your identity and purpose in the words of your Creator.

So how is it that the pain that enters my life is necessary? Well, for starters, pain is often the catalyst for growth in us. It is often in the painful seasons of our life that we learn something profound about ourselves. For many, what is learned is that we are often stronger than we give ourselves credit for, and we can take more than we previously thought. The thing that must be remembered is we have to allow ourselves time to grow and to learn life lessons through the discomforts we experience. Yes, God DOES love YOU too much to waste your pain!

The Bible teaches in Romans 8:28 (KJV), "And we know that all things work together for good to them that love God, to them who are the called according to His purpose." The key to this scripture being at work in your life is that you must be a believer and you must love God. With those two things in place, God is able to show you through your circumstances, good and bad, that He is sovereign. He is at work to use EVERYTHING you experience in this life to bring about something good in you. We often do not see the true testament of a person's character until we are tried by fire, lose a job, endure a failed marriage, experience the loss of a loved one, or have someone try and test our character. Never look at these things as trivial happenings but see them as opportunities to prove your love and devotion to God and to show a dying world how we should respond in the face of difficult situations. Remember, our God is intentional. Everything He does and allows has a divine purpose in the life of a believer. The key to operating in His divine order for our lives is to trust Him at His word. He never fails, and He uses our pains and discomforts to build our faith in Him. Keep trusting. It builds your faith! Keep trusting. It strengthens your resolve! Keep trusting. It pleases the heart of God! Keep trusting! Why? Simply put, because the fate of your soul is at stake!

Remember, do not despise God's process. Often, your biggest blessing comes in the guise of rejection, a layoff, or some other disappointment. Stay focused and prayerful. On the other side of the journey (God's process) is a blessing.

CHAPTER 5

The Power to Change Is in Your Mouth

Death and life are in the power of the tongue...

—Proverbs 18:21, KJV

There is an old adage in the secular arena that says, "In order to get help, you must first admit that there is a problem." To be quite honest, this saying can and should be applied to believers as well. However, in order for it to take hold and have a lasting effect in your life, we must take it a step further. We can admit we have a problem every day of the week, but until we make up our minds to DO something about it, then we will never be overcomers or victorious. Moreover, in order for us to see change, we often have to speak to those negative thought patterns that permeate our mind. We let destructive and negative thoughts live rent free in our heads while we try to cope with the physical, mental, and spiritual chaos they bring. We must bring those thoughts under subjection by speaking the Word of God to them. In addition, if we do not, we will continue to lose by default because we fail to activate our voice.

I am a firm believer in the fact that in order for you to understand who you are, where you are, and whose you are, you must know what the Word says. This means you must spend time reading it. The great thing about reading the Word is that it will speak to you about you. Because God is an intentional God, He will begin to open up your understanding as you begin to read His Word. God's Word is revelatory in that it comes in stages. You can receive a new understanding to something you have read many times over. This is what I like to refer to as a "layered" Word. God reveals to you as much as you are able to understand at any one sitting, and the ensuing revelation coincides with where you are in your walk with Him. He opens up the text to us in layers, allowing us to "digest" it in small bits and pieces so that we are able to get a fresh revelation—a new Word.

One such example for me is the book of Genesis, of which I have read many times. Genesis 1 chronicles the creation of the world and the creation of mankind. As God brings order to the chaos and disorder, the Bible says, "God said." The ensuing result of "God said" (stated ten times) is that the disorder obeyed God's directive and became what God said it would be. The revelatory Word that should be impressed upon our heart is this: whenever we are experiencing chaos and disorder in our lives, there are two things we must do. First, we must agree with what God says about it. Second, we have to SPEAK TO IT and tell it what it is to become even if that thing is YOU! Remember, God said in Genesis 1:3 (KJV), "Let there be light," and guess what? It became light. Just as God spoke to the thing He wanted to change, we are to do the same. Speak to those issues in your life, and then walk therein. I remember reading Mark 11:23, which says,

> For verily I say unto you, that whosoever shall say unto this mountain, Be thou removed, and be thou cast into the sea; and shall not doubt in his heart, but shall believe that those things which he saith shall come to pass; he shall have whatsoever he saith.
>
> —Mark 11:23, KJV

I had read this scripture many times in my lifetime, and it was not until I got older that I truly understood its meaning. This scripture signifies that we are to be atmosphere changers. We are to speak to those things in our lives that do not line up to the Word of God and tell them where they are to go or what they are to become. We are to stand on the promises of faith, speak the Word of God over our lives, and watch what it becomes. Notice the part of the scripture that reads that we are to "say" something. If you do not use your voice, you lose by default. For our lives to be in order, we must do what God says. We must speak to poverty and call it "abundance"; we must speak to fear and call it "power, love, and a sound mind." We must speak to death and call it "life." We must speak to loss and call it "victory." You see, when we speak to those things in our lives under the power and the authority of Jesus Christ, He will act on our behalf and prove Himself to us. Speak life and watch the Giver of Life change things on your behalf! Remember, He makes ALL things new!

CHAPTER 6
Your Identity Is in Christ

Therefore, if any man be in Christ, he is a new creature; old things are passed away; behold, all things are become new.

—2 Corinthians 5:17, KJV

I heard a preacher say in his sermon one day, "The created being is not greater than its creator." This saying has resonated within me for several years and has caused me to ponder my very identity, as it relates to my very presence in this world. Due to the situations I have endured over the course of my lifetime, I questioned my purpose, my value, and often times, my sanity. Even if you are a person who has a hard time believing that God exists, it would only make sense to believe there is a higher power in charge who is in control of what is placed in this universe. Case in point: let us look at a library. When you go to the library to check out a book or even to study, you do not think that something exploded, and books were the outcome of that explosion. You know that someone had to cut down trees to make paper, someone had to write the words, and someone had to operate the printing press. You see, someone had to manipulate all of these things in order for books to come into existence. So, I dare ask, "Why would you believe that the earth and everything in it was a random explosion that caused every breathing, living thing to occupy time and space in this world?"

So, what does that have to do with my identity in Christ? Well, for starters, in order to understand your identity in Christ, you must first believe that God exists. If you do not believe this fundamental truth, you are not going to be able to accept the fact that Christ is the Son of God, that He walked this earth for thirty-three years, and that He willingly went to the cross on your behalf. You will struggle with the fact that He rose on the third day, and that He sits at the right hand of the Father. If you are ever to find your identity and walk in the purpose God created you for, you must take those truths into your mind and sear them with a hot iron to your heart. There is no other truth that is greater than this: God is real.

Now that we know that we must first believe that God is real, we can look at how our belief in Him shapes our identity. When a child is created through sexual intercourse between his mother and father, DNA is passed through the blood. This blood carries the DNA that controls what a person will look like and shapes their personality. Often, as was my case, a child will hear, "You look just like your momma!" They may even tell the child, "You act just like your daddy!" They say these things because the DNA is at work in the child's life and has imprinted upon them. The same goes for believers when we accept Christ as our Lord and Savior. We are washed in His blood and are made into a new creation. Moreover, as we submit our will and ways to God and seek after Him, we become more like His Son, Jesus Christ.

Becoming more like Christ should be the one thing that we relentlessly chase after because Christ found favor in His Father's eyes. We should chase after Him more than money, the opposite sex, ambition, prestige, and/or fame. When God sees us, He sees Christ. Our lives should exemplify the fruits of the Spirit, which are "love, joy, peace, longsuffering, gentleness, goodness, faith, meekness, and temperance" (Galatians 5:22-23, KJV).

When you wholeheartedly pursue a relationship with God, everything about you begins to change. Your perception changes and causes you to see things through a changed mindset. As you yield more and more, your thought process changes, what comes out of your heart and mind changes, and your speech and motives change. I am convinced, now more than ever, that in order for us (I have not

Barbara Steger

arrived!) to see a difference in our lives and the lives of people we hold dear, we must connect to the person who is going to change our lives for the better. We must connect to the Creator and Maker of all living things. He knows everything about us because He created us. He knows the number of hairs on our head, and His thoughts of us are like grains of sand—they are bountiful and countless. The Word of God says this about God's thoughts towards us: "How precious also are thy thoughts unto me, O God! How great is the sum of them! If I should count them, they are more in number than the sand" (Psalm 139:17-18, KJV). Isn't it a good feeling to know that God is thinking of us non-stop? Even when we are not thinking about Him!

We must buy into the truth of God's Word. If you want to see yourself differently, you must see yourself through the Word of God. You must READ and ACCEPT what God says about you as the infallible truth. You are above and not beneath! You are the head and not the tail! You are blessed in your going in and your coming out! You are blessed in the city and in the fields! You are an overcomer! You are a friend of God! You are a member of the royal priesthood! You are a child of God! You are forgiven! You are made whole! You are healed! You are blessed! You are a new creation! YOU ARE WHAT AND WHO GOD SAYS YOU ARE!!

CHAPTER 7

Fear Is the Antithesis to Your Existence

For God has not given us the spirit of fear; but of power, and of love, and of a sound mind.

—2 Timothy 1:7, KJV

I do not know about you, but for a great portion of my life, fear walked me faithfully to every destination. Fear walked me to school, to church, to work, and it even walked with me into my marriage. Fear had a grip on both my thought process and my emotional stability. Fear would not dare let me dream, because to do so meant I would have to let go of certain beliefs and old paradigms that caused me to doubt my abilities. So it was fear that became the overbearing parent, and my dreams and desires became the child who had to ask permission to go anywhere and to do anything. And, as you probably already guessed, fear always said, "No!"

Fear was not just overbearing; fear was also a TERRIBLE parent. It shot me down every time I dared to dream, dared to soar, or even dared to be free. I was molested as a young child, and the fear that came from those events manifested as self-condemnation and shame. I could not seem to see myself as anything but the little girl whose trust had been broken and whose body had been violated. I learned to suppress my feelings, and for a long time, I mentally denied that those events even took place. I did not dare talk about it, because to do so meant the violation really happened and I deserved the treatment that I received. Fear bred self-hate and made me soft.

I did not have a voice then, and as I grew from a child into teenager, I did not know how to use my voice to silence my fear. Therefore, I went through life accepting whatever wrong people did to me—not because I liked it, but because fear taught me that I deserved it.

Fear made me believe that because I did not tell anyone about the violations done to me, that somehow it was my fault. My molester, the ADULT, told me not to tell anyone, so I did as I was told. Think about it—isn't obedience and respect for authority and adults what we are taught as children? I know! I was taught that by my parents too, and so, therein lies the conflict. I was only doing what I was taught to do, but somehow, fear convinced me it was my fault, and I was the guilty one. Pretty heavy for a little kid, huh? And to be honest, it was a guilt I carried well into my adulthood; to think, it wasn't ever mine to claim. But because I did not know any better, I claimed it and held it close like a small child does her favorite blanket or stuffed toy. The guilt became a part of my identity and shaped the way I handled the world—and more often than not, how I handled me.

Although I did not know the meaning of self-condemnation until I became much older, I recognize that I walked out a great portion of my life in it. After looking back and reflecting on the choices I have made over the years, I realized that self-condemnation is a by-product of fear, and it was driving my agenda. You see, because I had not yielded my life to Christ, sin was my nature. Every time I used my body to sin, especially sins of a sexual nature, I felt so much shame, but it was not enough to make me stop. And because I did not have Christ living on the inside of me, I did not have anything to help keep me from being promiscuous. It was a vicious cycle I kept repeating with no end seemingly in sight. Inevitably, I ended up violating myself again and again through my own destructive actions, not realizing that I was hurting my integrity, my name, and even my resolve. Remember this phrase: "Hurt people hurt people." In many of my situations, I was both the perpetuator and the victim.

Not only did I hurt, but those things forever changed the way I viewed people. It also made me afraid of everything and everyone. I did not make friends easily (something that I still struggle with today), and when I did, I only allowed people to get so close. I held them back using the invisible wall fear told me to erect. Fear said that I could not allow people to get too close or they would hurt me, shame me, judge me, and—yes, you guessed it—violate me. My rational then became that if I did not want to deal with those feelings, I had to make the choice to stay uninvolved, unattached, and uncommitted. This way of thinking harmed me in that I was alone so much because I did not want to connect with others, nor did I know how to do so. My self-imposed isolation caused me to become depressed and suicidal. My waking thoughts often included the scenario of "What if I was dead? Who would miss me?" I often believe that because my mother was a praying woman, she interceded for me even when I was not aware of her prayers. Her prayers kept me from harming myself and kept me alive so that I could walk out the plan God had created for me before I was even born.

It was not until I got older and grounded myself in the Word of God that I began to feel a release from the baggage of self-doubt and condemnation I had been carrying around for most of my life. When I got serious with God, God became my very present help in the TIMES of trouble. Yes, I wrote time with an "s" because my troubles were many. You see, God has always been serious about me, but because of my insecurities, frailties, faults, and fears, I could not see God. I could not see His path. I could not trace His hand. I could not trust His heart concerning me. As a result, I could not see God, in all of His magnificent splendor, loving someone like me.

The great thing about a story is that it has the ability to change the narration with each new addition of a page added to the end of a chapter, and it breathes new life back into the story. It works in very much the same way God does. God breathed on me, and my life (my story) began to change. He picked up the broken pieces of my heart and did reconstructive surgery. He took the jagged pieces of my heart, smoothed them out, and created a new heart. My new heart became soft and pliable to the will, heart, and mind of God; it began to function right, and it began to love right. And guess what love did? It kicked fear and all of its baggage out the door!

Declare this with me: fear will not be a part of my life. Depression is not allowed to coexist with me. The love of God compels everything that is tormenting me to leave, in Jesus' name. I am free! I am whole! I am LOVED!

CHAPTER 8

If You Live Long Enough, Disappointment Will Surely Come

...for he maketh his sun to rise on the evil and on the good, and sendeth rain on the just and on the unjust.

—Matthew 5:45, KJV

Disappointment is an inevitable part of life we all will experience, no matter how morally good or saved we are. All people from every walk of life and from every race, creed, nationality, and origin will experience events in their lives that will leave them disappointed with people, places, and things. Things will happen to cause even the holiest saint to question her abilities, her dedication, her sanity, and even—get this—her faith in God. Yes, REALLY. Some things, circumstances, and people will rock you to your core and leave you looking crazy, acting crazy, and thinking crazy if you let them. If you allow the disappointment to take up space in your heart, it will fester and ooze like an infected wound left untreated and to the elements around it. You get the picture. It becomes nasty and will infect good tissue around it if you do not take measures and use preventive medicine. Not dealing with the disappointment will leave you unable to process your emotions effectively. Bitterness, anger, and self-pity will become your BFFs if you allow your emotions and thoughts to go unchecked. If you are to walk in the favor of God, you must find ways to guard your heart at all times. Proverbs 4:23 (KJV) teaches us to "Keep thy heart with all diligence; for out of it are the issues of life."

The problem with not confronting disappointment when it confronts you is that you cannot go further in this journey in a positive manner. When there is no maturation, people are bound to repeat the same mistakes because their thinking hasn't changed. Before your actions ever change in the way that you handle something, there must be a change in your perception. Often, it is said that a person's perception is their reality. What a person perceives (believes, understands, or feels) about a thing ultimately determines how they react to it. If we are to do better, we must think better, and we do that by submitting our thoughts to our heavenly Father. The Bible teaches us this in 2 Corinthians 10:5 (KJV), which states we are "Cast[ing] down imaginations, and every high thing that exalteth itself against the knowledge of God, and bringing into captivity every thought to the obedience of Christ."

If we are to fully function without dysfunction, then we must learn to make our thoughts heed the Word of God. Think about it this way, if we hang out with a person who is negative and NEVER has a positive word to say about anything or anybody, we tend to find their presence taxing on our soul and inner peace. Well, the same is applied to your thought process. The more we listen to the enemy and our inner-me, the more our spiritual walk and our inner peace is disturbed. If left unchecked (us not using our voice to speak to the situation), we will succumb to the voice that tells us that we are not God's children. And the truth of the matter is this: you will know it is the enemy's voice because he will always remind you of some past mistake, fall, habit, or sin. He will try to make you believe you are not forgiven and are a failure in your walk with Christ. Isn't it funny how God always speaks to us as our future selves, but Man keeps speaking to us from who and what we used to be before Christ? We have to remember that in Christ we are a NEW creation. Who we used to be and what we used to do ceases to exist anymore. Just like God changed Abram's name and he became Abraham, the father of many nations, God will do the same for us. And in order to walk in God's favor authentically and full of power, we must learn to stop answering to our old name. You get to choose WHAT and WHO you answer to. I choose to answer to the Giver and Sustainer of life because He has an excellent plan for my life. Even though there might be fog all around me making my path unsure, I know God's Word "is a lamp unto my feet, and a light unto my path" (Psalm 119:105, KJV). When I keep my thoughts on Him, he will make sure I am walking in His power, in His might, and in His favor.

Declaration time: I choose to believe the Word of God, and I know that God loves me unconditionally. I denounce the words that have been spoken to me, whispered to me, and even written to me which say I am worthless or that my life does not have meaning. Today, I choose to answer to God and the names He has given to me. I am royal priesthood. I have been chosen and redeemed. I am a friend of God. The old me doesn't live here anymore. I have been forever changed by the renewing of my mind.

CHAPTER 9
You Are Never Alone

Whither shall I go from thy Spirit? or whither shall I flee from thy presence? If I ascend up into heaven, thou art there; If I make my bed in hell, behold, thou art there; If I take the wings of the morning, and dwell in the uttermost parts of the sea; even there shall thy hand lead me, and thy right hand shall hold me.

—Psalm 139:7-10, KJV

One of the hardest concepts for me to grasp as a small child was the fact that God was omnipresent. The capacity of my childlike mind could not fathom that if God could be everywhere, why was it that my parents could not? I likened God to have the attributes of the moon, because when I went outside at night, it was if it were following me. I could see the moon from every vantage point, which meant it could see me too. My baby boy, André, would say all the time when he was three or four that the moon was following him and that it scared him.

My thoughts about God were pretty much along those lines. When I became older and rationalized that He was present all the time and everywhere, the sins and hurts of my past caused me to want to slink away from God's presence. You see, self-condemnation had a vice-grip on my emotions and fear. It was my over-bearing parent, and it would not let me make the choice to believe the best about myself. It always told me how to feel (scared), how to think (negative), and how to live (dysfunctional). I struggled with my faith, and I struggled with the thought that a God who is so righteous, holy, and good could love someone like me. And the thing is this, I ran from the face and voice of God so many times.

It wasn't until I came to myself that I realized God didn't just have the answer to my problems, but that He was and still is the answer to everything that plagues me. It wasn't until that realization settled in my heart that I was able to truly let go and let God. I was able to find my place and my strength in Him. And, if I am to be totally honest and transparent, even now there are times that I get weak in my faith, and I don't pray or read my Bible like I ought to. Often, I think negatively about myself and feel unqualified. I realize I am not perfect, and I often fall short of God's unmerited grace, mercy, and favor. And here lately, life has handed out some disappointments, things that have had me question at times "Why me?" I've even gone into prayer only to weep before the Lord out of pain. But the great thing about having a relationship with God is that He hears, knows, and understands what I—we—are going through. When I cannot find the words to articulate what is in my heart, the Holy Spirit takes over and articulates it for me. No, you are not weak for weeping before the Lord. Trust me, it is exactly the opposite. When you can cry and moan before God, you are acknowledging that He is the source of your joy and strength. When you then tell Him to "Have your way in my life, Lord" in spite of the difficulties that you are presently facing, that is when you know that you are growing and maturing in the Lord.

Don't be afraid to share all of you with your Savior. Why? Because there is NOTHING hidden from Him. He knows your heart anyways. And to put things into perspective, if it were easy to trust God in the midst of uncertainty, everybody would be doing it. Trusting in times when you cannot see your way is WORK! We have to remember that our God never leaves us nor forsakes us, and if we are to be victorious in our walk with Christ, we will have to work our faith. When working your faith, don't be surprised when it seems like all hell has broken loose. When you decide to trust that God is truly for you and you are seeking Him with every fiber of your being, the enemy will come in like a wrecking ball. He will do everything in his power to make you think trusting God is a useless activity and everything was better before you did. Don't believe the hype! He does not want that seed of determination to take root in your heart because he knows that when it does, you will move from being a mediocre Christian to a Christian who is sold-out to the things of God. A Christian full of the power, authority, anointing, and the favor of God. Don't let what your eyes see cause you to miss your destiny. God is always with you, and He fights for you!

CHAPTER 10
Child-like Faith

Then were there brought unto him little children that
he should put his hands on them, and pray: and the
disciples rebuked them. But Jesus said, Suffer little children, and forbid them not, to come unto me: for of
such is the kingdom of heaven.

—Matthew 19:13-14, KJV

I am a firm believer that in order for others to be helped, it is important that people are transparent in their struggles. It is not necessary
to divulge every minute detail, but it is important for others to understand they are not alone, others have experienced the same types
of struggles, and they have overcome.

One day, I was particularly overwhelmed, and I was not in a good
place emotionally. Some things had unsettled my spirit, and I was
having a rough time dealing with the situation that presented itself.
Although I can usually find the right words in most situations, when
I am perplexed about something, I am not expressive, because I then
internalize EVERYTHING and shut down emotionally. I went to
church that morning, and the pastor preached an awesome sermon
centered on God being a covenant keeper. My heart was heavy when
I arrived at church, and although the man of God preached a dy-
namic word, my heart was still heavy when church was over. There
was such a stronghold on my emotions that I could not feel God's
presence, although people were rejoicing in the Spirit all around me.
Normally, I can talk to my mom when I am down and instantly feel

better. However, on that day, after speaking with her, I still felt the same. I went to bed heavy-hearted that night and woke up the same way.

I used to watch my grandbaby, Sebastian, on the weekends so his mom could go to work. As is my usual custom, I play gospel music while I am cleaning the house, and that day was no exception except for the fact Sebastian was really excited when the music began to play. He told me he wanted to praise and worship Jesus with me. I said, "Okay," but continued to clean. He then said, "Come on, Grandma! We need to go pray in your closet" with so much excitement. I listened to my little buddy, and we went to the closet, kneeled on some pillows, and clasped our hands together on top of the bench that was there. I began to pray audibly as I have always done when we pray together. As I prayed, Bash began repeating the words in his little baby voice. He also prayed the words with the same intensity and fervor that I gave them. He then asked God to bless his mom, without me saying it first. That baby loves his momma! He then raised his hands to the ceiling and began to worship, saying things like, "Hallelujah!" and "Thank you, Jesus!" Because of Bash's enthusiasm for praise, prayer, and worship, he helped me to take the focus off the problem and off myself, and he also helped to align my thoughts on our heavenly Father.

Needless to say, I was reminded that we must approach the throne of grace like a little child and learn to trust God through the good and the bad, the ups and the downs. The things troubling my spirit became so small during our worship time, and I was able to put them exactly where they needed to be—at the feet of Jesus. I realized I had been sick, tired, and mentally exhausted for weeks, and I was feeling like my life was spiraling out of control. My life was beginning to feel unbalanced, and although I had committed and disciplined myself to get up at 4:00 am for prayer, even that was beginning to feel like a chore. I did not have Sebastian's excitement about talking to God anymore, and I knew that I needed an intervention of sorts. I needed deliverance from my thought life because it was causing me to believe the situation I was going through was bigger than the God that I serve.

When I think back fondly on that day, I am reminded that others may look at our lives and think we have it all together. They think that because we look the part, we do not experience hardship, loneliness, disappointments, or pain. The truth of the matter is that we do, and it is what we do with those emotions that becomes the key to our survival and the restoration of our faith. We must give those things and our worship to God so that He can do what only He can do. He will heal us from the inside and help us to put the issues of our heart into perspective. As Christians, we have to believe the Word of God when it says, "Many are the afflictions of the righteous; but the Lord delivereth him out of them all" (Psalm 34:19, KJV). The Hebrew word for affliction is "'oniy" and the definition means "misery" or "burden." The image is that of someone bowed down by a heavy burden. However, because God is a covenant keeper, as His children we can rest assured knowing He knows, He cares, and He understands, and He will also work things out on our behalf for His purpose and His glory.

I thanked God for my grandson on that day. He taught me how to truly worship God in spite of how I was feeling. Sometimes, as adults we need reminding, even if it comes from a two-and-a-half-year-old.

Declare this with me: no matter what my present-day circumstances look or feel like, I will trust in the Lord. God is bigger than my problems, and He will bring me through. My Father, God, wants to show His heart towards me.

CHAPTER 11

Being Sold Out Will Cost You

But all these things they will they do unto you for my name's sake, because they know not him that sent me.

—John 15:21, KJV

One of the biggest misconceptions that Christians have is the belief that when they give their life to Christ, they will experience a trouble-free life until they die or are raptured. This could not be further from the truth! The problem with this thinking is that not only is it untrue, but it isn't even biblical. For the Bible teaches us in Psalm 34:19 (KJV) that "many are the afflictions of the righteous: but the Lord delivereth him out of them all." We are going to experience some hard times, and we may have to cry sometimes, but we can rest knowing that we are favored of God. He will deliver us—even from things we often bring on ourselves out of ignorance and willful disobedience. In this Christian walk, rejection is something that we will experience at some point in our lives. No matter who you are, how old or young you are, and what position or status you hold, you will ultimately experience rejection and persecution. And while these things do not feel good, it is often necessary for our social and spiritual growth. Think of it this way—what doesn't kill you will make you stronger.

Webster's dictionary defines rejection this way: it is to refuse to accept, refuse to consider, use or submit to.[iii] It also means to throw out, refuse to hear, or refuse to receive of or grant admittance to. It also could mean to rebuff or to withhold love from. With all the negative verbiage surrounding this word, it is no wonder we have a problem with being rejected, sometimes to the extent we will straddle the fence instead of staying true to our convictions and religious beliefs. We often do and say things that are in direct opposition to our character so that we will be accepted by the masses. Why? Because it is human nature to want to fit in and belong. God created us with an innate want and need for companionship from others. In fact, in the garden of Eden after the creation of Man, God states in Genesis 2:18 (KJV) that "it is not good that the man should be alone. I will make a help meet for him." Of course, we know God created woman so that Adam would not be lonely, but he also created Eve as Adam's friend and partner for life. And so it is with us today; people want, need, and value friendship. In fact, it is healthy to have friends, but we must use wisdom and discernment to make sure we have linked up with the right people. Even in our friendships, it is important for us to be equally yoked. When we make up in our minds to follow Jesus and walk authentically in His favor, we will experience difficulties in our relationships. Living lives that mirror Christ's redemptive work in us causes us to encounter rejection.

Everyone will experience rejection at some point in their life; however, some seem to experience it less than others. For many of us, especially those of us with vibrant and colorful personalities, we are the life of the party. For people like that, making friends is never hard to do. In fact, we have met little children who seem not to notice a person's body size, skin color, or even their handicaps and flaws; they simply have a joy for life and want to say "Hi!" to everyone they meet. Their mothers may even venture to say Little Johnny or Mary never meets a stranger. These people tend to float through life having a seemingly endless number of friends. Everywhere they go, the "turn-up" is in effect, the party will be happening, and the talk of what went down the day after the party provides details that legends are made of. In fact, these gatherings would be called epic. These people could have a falling out with an individual and can normally patch things up fairly quickly. They are able to become friends again with the other person easily, even if they are the offending party. They are able to do so simply because they are popular, attractive, funny, gifted, and/or outgoing. People want to stay connected to people like that. People like being connected to the Social Butterfly, because being connected to people like that somehow makes people feel better about themselves.

However, may I dare say that one of the fastest ways to lose friends and to stay unfriended is to be totally committed to walking with God? To get really saved and be sold out for the Lord? Being sold out means that you have taken your eyes off the things of this world and have turned to Jesus with all of your heart; you now hunger and thirst for righteousness. You become more concerned about what God thinks about you than what the people around you think. And for many, this new change about you, this new you, stands in stark contrast to the person you once were. The Bible asks the question in Amos 3:3 (KJV), "Can two walk together except they be agreed?" We know that they cannot walk together from point A to point B unless they are likeminded and have the same goal in mind. As children, our parents would often say, "Birds of a feather flock together." We took this to mean that people of the same mind usually hung out together in social groups. Jocks hung with other athletes; students who were very studious usually hung out with other students who were just as conscientious about their schoolwork. And so it is with our declaration of faith. The Bible teaches us in Hebrews 10:25 (KJV) to "not forsake the assembling of ourselves together as the manner of some is; but exhorting one another." Why? Because God knows that in order for us to stay saved, walk in strength, and be empowered by the encouraging words of others, we need to hang around like-minded people in the faith. When you declare you want to live like the Christians Paul talks about in Romans 12:1-2, you will find yourself being rejected by the people you once walked with and broke bread with.

Romans 12: 1-2 says,

I beseech you, therefore, brethren, by the mercies of

God, that ye present your bodies a living sacrifice, holy, acceptable unto God, which is your reasonable service. (2) And be not conformed to this world: but be ye transformed by the renewing of your mind, that ye may prove what is that good, and acceptable, and perfect, will of God.

—Romans 12: 1-2, KJV

And because you have embraced this scripture as it relates to your relationship with Christ, you will find that your so called "friends" no longer enjoy being in our presence. Why? Because they are no longer comfortable around you anymore, and also because the God in you makes the devil in them uncomfortable, because light always exposes darkness. All of a sudden, they have these cute little names they refer to you as, such as "Religious Fanatic," "Jesus-Freak," "Holy Roller," or "one of them," and ultimately, because the sin nature loves darkness more than they love the light, you will experience the ramifications of being rejected. Once you become serious about spiritual matters, the people in your inner circle, your bestie, and even your unsaved family members will begin to view you differently. Be taking your eyes off the things of this world, and by turning to Jesus with all of your heart, you will be rejected. You see, when you get focused on pleasing God, you will begin to pull down the idols you have exalted higher than Christ—the idols of fame, money, material possessions, our children, spouses, our jobs, and anything and everything we have made more important than Jesus.

When you go all the way with God, you begin to dig deeper into God's Word, searching for more of His truth. You stop pursuing material possessions and become obsessed with pursuing God. We often sing the song "Chasing After You" by Vashawn Mitchell, whose lyrics say, "I'm chasing after you, no matter what I have to do 'cause I need you more and more." But do we really mean it? Do we really mean that we will do whatever it takes? Because when you become sold out, your friends and family may begin to think you are crazy. Instead of rejoicing with you or encouraging you to continue to walk with the Lord, they say things like, "Girl! What's the matter with you?" or "Have you lost your mind?" They will even say the all-too-familiar, "Baby, it doesn't take all of that." But I want to let you know that yes, it does take all of that and then some! Being a disciple of Jesus Christ comes with a price. And YES, as a Christian, we will be rejected and persecuted, and yes, we should expect it. So the question herein is, "What does the Bible say about it?

In order to deal with rejection properly, we must understand why rejection takes place in the life of a believer. John 16:18-21 gives us Jesus' words as he talks about rejection (and persecution), because these two things often go hand-in-hand. There are some things we must bear in mind:

1. We are rejected because we are no longer identified with the world. John 15:18 (KJV) says, "If the world hate you, ye know that it hated me before it hated you." The world does not love anything that is not inherently its own. John 3:19-20 (KJV) says, "And this is the condemnation (verdict), that light is come into the world, and men loved darkness rather than light, because their deeds were evil. For every one that doeth evil hateth the light, neither cometh to the light, lest his deeds should be reproved." Your new life in Christ be-comes a spiritual threat to those people around you who do not know Christ. Romans 12:2 (NLT), a familiar passage of scripture tells us "Do not copy the behavior and cus-toms of the world, but let God transform you into a new person by changing the way you think. Then you will learn God's will for you, which is good and pleasing and perfect." The Bible also teaches in 2 Corinthians 5:17 that once we accept Christ, we have been changed: "Therefore, If any man be in Christ, he is a new creature: old things are past away; behold, all things are become new" (KJV). So often

when a person has changed, people will say, "You are acting brand new," and in the case of a believer, he or she is new. Therefore, the unbeliever, especially one he or she has spent lots of time with, can no longer identify with the person's new character. Thus, setting the non-believer at odds with the child of God. So, in essence, it is not the saint they are rejecting, it is the God nature being manifested in the life of the believer that they have a problem with. Remember, it is better to be loved than to be liked. Essentially what this statement means in a spiritual context is it is better to experience Jesus' unconditional and unchanging love for us than to be popular and loved by the world.

2. We are identified with Christ, and our lives should reflect His character and His calling. John 15:20 (KJV) says, "Remember the word that I said unto you, The servant is not greater than his lord. If they have persecuted me, they will also persecute you; if they kept my saying, they will keep yours too." Because Christians do not belong to the world, rejection and persecution from the world is inevitable. And the definition of inevitable is "certain to happen, and unavoidable."[iv] The basic reason why this occurs is because of the world's ignorance and rejection of God the Father. As a matter of fact, we should not be in shock when we go through things. 1 Peter says,

> Beloved, think it not strange concerning the fiery trial which is to try you, as some strange thing happened unto you: (13) But rejoice, inasmuch as ye are partakers of Christ's sufferings; that, when his glory shall be revealed, ye may be glad also with exceeding joy. (14) If ye be reproached for the name of Christ, happy are ye; for the spirit of glory and of God resteth upon you:

on their part he is evil spoken of, but on our part he is glorified. (15) But let none of you suffer as a murderer, or as a thief, or as an evildoer, or as a busybody in other men's matters. (16) Yet, if any man suffer as a Christian, let him not be ashamed; but let him glorify God on this behalf.

1 Peter 4:12-16, KJV

Based on this scripture text, we should approach our trials, persecutions, and rejections with gladness because God is being glorified when we handle these things appropriately. The enemy will have you to believe when you are going through situations that you have done something wrong. However, if you know you are walking in spiritual integrity, then it is just the opposite. The attacks normally come because you are doing something right—you have become a threat to the enemy and his demons. When we go through standing in God's truth and in the power of His might, we make God proud, and we show the naysayers that our God is bigger than anything we face. Because we are now identified with God through Christ Jesus, we are His children. And because we are His children, that relationship guarantees us some basic rights. Although persecuted and rejected, God loves us with an everlasting love, and He will protect us.

3. They will reject us because they don't know God. John 15:21 (KJV) says, "But all these things will they do unto you for my name's sake, because they know not Him that sent me." In this day and age, it is not uncommon for people to say they are Christian. And although to be a Christian is to be Christ-like in thought, deed, and speech, many live their lives devoid of any real connection to Christ. What we have

are people who have some knowledge of who God is, but they do not know Him—they do not have a relationship. And because they do not have a covenantal relationship with God, their lives are full of sin, which is represented by darkness. Because their lives are full of darkness, they cannot coexist with light because light pervades the darkness and exposes everything hidden therein. So, when you receive Christ and you grow stronger in your walk, your light will condemn the darkness that is ever-present in the life of a sinner, whether it be a friend or family member. Again, the Holy Ghost in you will have tried the spirit by the spirt in them and will find that they are not of God. And the flip side to that is the spirit working within that individual will try itself against the spirit of God in you. Because the enemy hates God, he cannot help but to hate God's most prized possession, which is mankind, and especially when a person has found their identity in Christ.

Remember: believing Jesus Christ is the way, the truth and the life, being unashamed of the Gospel, holding firm to eternal truths and convictions, and taking up our cross to follow Christ will put us at odds with the world and its standards. Friendship with Jesus comes with a hefty price tag; it will cost us the world's hatred of us. However, great is your reward if you keep your heart fixed on Jesus Christ.

> Blessed are ye, when men shall hate you, and when they shall separate you from their company, and shall reproach you, and cast out your name as evil, for the Son of man's sake. (23) Rejoice ye in that day, and leap for joy; for behold, your reward is great in heaven: for in like manner did their fathers unto the prophets.
>
> —Luke 6:22-23, KJV

Barbara Steger

Walking in the favor of God does not mean that we won't experience rejection or persecution, but what it does mean is that we have a heavenly Father who is faithful and just, and He will protect us from any weapon that is formed against us.

CHAPTER 12

Identity Crisis

Hear me. O Lord, hear me, that this people may know that thou art the Lord God, and that thou hast turned their heart back again.

—I Kings 18:37, KJV

Webster's Dictionary defines "Identity" as "who you are, the way you think about yourself, the way you are viewed by the world and the characteristics that define you."[v] In this worldly perspective, we can liken identity to the concept of self-esteem, which ultimately says, "How I feel about myself is how I will react to the world around me, and ultimately how I will treat myself and others." Now, I don't know about you, but to me, there is something fundamentally and foundationally wrong when we apply this mindset as a believer. Why? Because everything about that definition is rooted in the sufficiency of "Me, myself, and I." It often bases our dealings with the natural world on false information, alternative facts (LIES!), misrepresentations, deceptive practices, and just plain wrong thinking. It is characterized by a thought process that has gone AWOL (Absent Without Leave) and a lifestyle that has gone rogue (out here doing life on my own, independent of God the Father), without any accountability.

And so it is that when our mind's thoughts are left unchecked, we find ourselves living in a spiritually dry place...we become shipwrecked, desolate, stagnate, and even desperate. And it is because of the damage that is done to our walk that the Bible teaches us that we are to bring every thought into captivity to the obedience of Christ. We are to make our thoughts recognize and obey the Word of the

Lord. When we fail to take control over our thought life, it causes us to view ourselves from dirty lenses, causing us to see things that aren't there. Because our viewpoint is cloudy, we often view ourselves incorrectly. This is causing us to have a distorted view, which triggers us to experience an identity crisis. An identity crisis is defined as a "period of uncertainty and confusion in which a person's identity becomes insecure, typically due to a change of direction in their expected aims or role in society."[vi] For believers, this change occurs in their role in the body of Christ.

In I Kings 19: 2-4, we are introduced to the prophet Elijah. He had just come off a major showdown in which he challenged Jezebel's prophets to a battle of the gods. This is a very familiar passage of Scripture, one in which when it is preached normally focuses on the spectacular performance of God displayed om Mt. Carmel. Elijah stands alone against 450 of Jezebel's Baal prophets and 400 prophets of Asherah, and he declares that God is the one true and living God. Can you imagine the faith it must've taken to be the lone voice declaring God is God, and He alone reigns in the midst of so many who did not believe? What a daunting task! I often question myself as to whether I would have had the courage to stand against Jezebel and the prophets and declare God's sovereignty. If you continue to read the chapter, you will see that after God displays His might, Elijah, who was walking and operating with the favor of God on his life, executed all of Jezebel's prophets. How many of you know that there is no anger like a woman who wants her way and cannot get it!

A little later in that chapter, we see that Jezebel declares a word curse and says that she is going to kill Elijah for the execution of her prophets. Elijah becomes fearful (there goes our foe FEAR again!), even after being used by God in such a powerful way. His view and his impact shifted, and instead of holding fast to the faithfulness of God's character, he panics, runs, and hides. I don't know about you, but this has been the narrative of my life. In times of fear, I have often run and hid from my problems and the face of God. Elijah forgot WHOSE he was, and in that moment, experiences an emotional breakdown and has an identity crisis—much like many of us today. We get so focused on what is being said about us, that we forget what God has already said about us (as I am typing this out, God is convicting my heart!). We get so focused on what others say we can't do that we forget about what God has already done through us. We begin to look at ourselves differently based on the fear that we let permeate our thought process. And who we are has NEVER been a question.

The Bible clearly states God's heat—his intentions towards us. Jeremiah 29:11 clearly defines that for us. We often times forget that God knows the thoughts He thinks towards us and those thoughts are of peace and not evil to give us a hope and a future. Ultimately, how we perceive ourselves should come from a Christ-centered mindset, and we should see ourselves in light of what God has already said about us. The fact that He says we are more than conquerors, the righteous of God, and the friend of God should help remind us of who are in Him. Our identity comes from knowing that we are His children, and our sense of worth comes from our commitment to be like His Son, Jesus Christ.

You see, Elijah allowed the enemy to toy with his emotions. Elijah was in his feelings. He allowed Jezebel's words to cause fear and overtake his rationale. He forgot in that moment God is all powerful. He forgot God promised that He would never leave him or forsake him. He forgot the miraculous feat that God displayed openly only a day or so before. He forgot who he was and whose he was. Elijah had an identity crisis, and if we are to be honest, we can say that we have been just like Elijah. We have allowed Sister So-and-So and Brother What-Not to make us believe we do not measure up. We allow others' opinions to shape and mold how we feel about ourselves. We allow the voice of the enemy to speak louder than the voice of the Lord. We start seeing ourselves through the mistakes and the hurts of our past, just as Elijah did. We panic, run, and hide, and we start acting in a manner that is not consistent to who we are. We begin to doubt and question our unique giftings, talents, and the call that is on our life—even though it has been confirmed time and time again. We begin to step back when we should be stepping up. We become silent when we should be crying out. We become despondent when we should be declaring and decreeing some things over our lives. We are in the midst of an identity crisis.

We often live like spiritual paupers because we focus on the mechanics of Christianity instead of a relationship with the Lord. We attend Bible study, give our tithes and offerings, serve on various committees, but if the truth be told, many of us are walking around devoid of any real power. We have become the walking wounded; we are MIA (Missing in Action); we are spiritually broken and have taken to the wearing of masks to hide the brokenness of our lives. When asked how we are doing, instead of telling the truth about how we feel, we offer up the ever-popular cliché:' "I am blessed and highly favored." And for the most part, those words don't carry the truth in our hearts. They have become words we say to sound spiritual.

When we should say that we are hurting, instead we say, "How can I help you?" It is perfectly alright to assist and be a blessing to others; however, we cannot continue to grow and maturate if we give and give and are never replenished. It only makes sense that if it is God's desire that all be saved and none lost, the "all" includes you too. God wants you to be free too!

For many of us, accepting that God wants to deliver and set us free is hard to do. The truth of the matter is that we can often give a positive and uplifting word to someone about their situation, but we can't speak a word of peace to the storm that is wreaking havoc in our own lives! God wants us to help others, but He wants you to be free too! If we wish to enjoy all that has been given to us through our covenant relations, we must not only delight ourselves in the Word, but we must see ourselves in God's Word. We must identify with the truth of God's Word as it relates to how He, God the Father, sees us.

Even with the awesome power God displayed and used through Elijah to facilitate, Elijah allowed the words of Jezebel the prophet to drive him to isolation. We often do the same. We must be careful as to who we allow to speak into our lives, because if we are not rooted and grounded in the sufficiency of who God is and what He means to us, we will find ourselves questioning our identities in Christ. Eve, in the garden of Eden, allowed the serpent to speak to her and made her doubt the sufficiency of God. All that she had been given to sustain her life and soul had been provided by God, yet the enemy was able to make her think God was withholding something from her—thus her conversation with the serpent was the catalyst to the fall of mankind. She doubted who she was and doubted her role in the world. Eve, and subsequently, Adam, had an identity crisis. They both wanted to be something God did not create them to be. Because of this illicit desire to be something they were not, they disobeyed God by eating the forbidden fruit.

I cannot state enough that in Christ we become a new creation. Our identity changed and so did our name. When we accepted Christ, our name changed from sinner to saint, from lost to found, from cursed to blessed, and from rejected to highly favored. You get the picture—our identity changes; however, we cannot forget how Eve was deceived. In order to gain a foothold in our lives, the enemy begins to attack our minds, just as he did to Eve. He begins to call you by your old name, your old sin. He begins to remind you how you used to act and the things you used to like. He reminds you of the things that hurt you in the past—the divorce, the molestation, the bitter break-up, the lost job. He causes you to rehearse those situations over and over again in your mind because he knows they are emotional triggers that will cause you to be like Elijah. He is hoping that you will become panicked, that you will run away from your calling, and that you will hide your talents and your giftings. He is hoping that you will refuse to be used by God, and so, the thing we must do is not to answer to our old name and those old shames. You see, Abram became Abraham, and he became the father of many nations. Saul, a persecutor of the saints, became Apostle Paul and is considered one who was a staunch supporter of Christ and helped to establish the church. So, you see, you have to wonder what is the enemy trying to kill in this season of your life? What is he trying to silence in this hour?

I am reminded of the story of Hannah, which can be found in I Samuel. A man name Elkanah had two wives, Penninah and Hannah. His wife Penninah was able to birth him sons and daughters, but his wife Hannah was barren. But the Bible says Elkanah LOVED Hannah. Penninah would provoke and vex Hannah to the point of tears and depression because of her inability to produce a child. So, I ask, "Why the attacks against your mind? Why does the enemy send people your way to cause you inner turmoil?" Well for starters, the enemy doesn't want you produce what God says you can produce. He knows that if he can defeat your mind, he can stop what is to be birthed through you. Hannah's story doesn't end there, though. She gets over her depression, petitions God for a son, and God grants her heart's desire. He becomes Samuel, the prophet. You never know what is to be birthed through you when you get your heart and mind in alignment to God's Word. Hannah goes on to have five more children, and to think she was depressed about being barren! You see, as long as she answered to her barrenness, Hannah remained without a child. It wasn't until she refocused her thoughts that she was able to birth that which God ordained.

Saints of God, the enemy may call us by our old names, but we don't have to answer. Refuse to have an identity crisis and remind the enemy and anyone else who attempts to call you by your old name that "so and so" doesn't live here anymore. And NO, she or he did not leave a forwarding address! We are the righteousness of God, and if we are to do and be anything in Christ Jesus, we must refuse to be tormented in our minds, and we have to want to be free. I am convinced now more than ever that the reason some of us repeat cycles of highs and lows in our lives is because we are not willing to truly be free. For so long, the hurts of our past have defined who we are—that is a pain we understand and are familiar with. This is a place that we have been comfortable with being in because it has been with us for so long. We have used those hurts and pains to shape our perceptions and, ultimately, our reality about people and things. And so, we hold onto the pain like a little child holding onto her favorite blanket. We hold on tightly. Refusing to let go and come out of bondage, refusing to be free, and refusing to be everything God has created us to be. But the devil is a liar! I decree and declare that as you are reading this chapter that this is your set time to be free in the mighty name of Jesus! His shed blood makes us free, and we will allow the blood to reach those places that have fortified walls. Tell yourself you are free and say it like you mean it! We have to serve the devil notice that fear doesn't live here anymore!

One way to do that is to stop walking in despondency and despair. Many of us do as Elijah did—upon hearing a troubling word about a certain situation, he becomes depressed. We begin to mope around the house. We stop taking care of ourselves. Some of us stop bathing and eating. We start sleeping all the time, and someone has to tell us to get up. We have become despondent. How do I know Elijah became this way? Well, in the Word, I King 19:4-7 (KJV) says, "But he himself went a day's journey into the wilderness [he isolated himself], and came and sat down under a juniper tree; and he requested for himself that he might die: [he had a pity party and is suicidal] and said, It is enough; now Oh Lord, take away my life; for I am not better than my fathers." He's talking crazy. Elijah is having a full-blown identity crisis. 1 King 19:5 (KJV) goes on to say that as he slept, an angel came and told him to "arise and eat." Then, in 1 King 19:7 (KJV), the angel tells him again to "arise and eat." So, I ask you, doesn't that sound like some of us?

At one point in my Christian walk, that was me. I had very high highs and very low lows in my walk with Christ, all because I did not apply the Word for myself. I wasn't praying for myself, and I wasn't talking to God for myself. It wasn't until I got sick and tired of being sick and tired that Baal Parazim, the God of the Breakthrough, brought my breakthrough. I had to get tired of holding on to the pain of molestation I experienced as a young child. I had to let go of the pain associated with my rape at the age sixteen when someone drugged my drink at a party. I had to let go of the guilt and shame I felt from living a promiscuous life in my youth. I had to forgive myself for the adultery I brought to my marriage. I had to let go of some stuff because, just like Elijah, I wanted to die. LITERALLY. I wanted to end it all, but something on the inside of me rose up, and I had to be like David and encourage myself. Something rose up on the inside of me and caused me to cry out to the Author and Finisher of my faith. It caused me to rise up and truly EAT the Word of the Lord. I began to apply the Word of the Lord, and the Word of the Lord began to work for me.

My attitude about those hurtful things I experienced changed. I remember even asking God during my identity crisis, "Why me?" And the answer I got from God was, "Why not you?" I had to realize in that moment the things I experienced really weren't about the past me; they were about the future me. We've got to change our thought process and believe without a shadow of a doubt that our God is an intentional God, and that the things we go through will bring about a transition—a process that will push us into the plan of God for our lives. Those things will catapult us into our destiny. Those things will help us be relatable, and we can say to our sister and brother, "Me too! But let me show you how God resurrected and transformed my life." Once we can let go of the baggage that comes from those instances, we can use those circumstances to minister. People need to know that they are not alone, and people need to know they can live a victorious Christ-centered life after experiencing pain. God loves you too much to waste your pain. He uses it all to bring about the good He has predestined for us. We just have to be in agreement with God's Word and will as it pertains to us. We are not cursed. We are blessed and highly favored of God!

The Bible teaches us in Proverbs 18:21 (KJV) that "Death and Life are in the power of the tongue." We must start resisting the devil and putting him to flight. We must open our mouths to decree and declare some things over our lives if we want to live and operate in the favor of God.

Declare this with me: I decree and declare that I am free from the pains of my past. In Christ, I have become a new person, and I will no longer answer to the names others have labeled me. I release myself from any negative words spoken over my life by others and even those negative words I have spoken over myself. I will be all that You have created me to be, and I will rest in Your grace and mercy. I am free, delivered, and restored!

In Jesus' name, Amen!

CHAPTER 13

Prayer is the Key

If my people which are called by my name, shall humble themselves, and pray, and seek my face, and turn from their wicked ways; then will I hear from heaven, and will forgive their sin, and will heal their land.

—2 Chronicles 7:14, KJV

I have always been a person who likes to read a lot. And because I enjoy reading, I find myself reading and researching things that intrigue me or even those things that plague me. Because of this, my brothers and friends have often called me a "nerd." One of the things that has intrigued me is this thing called Prayer. I have made it my mission to understand what it is, its purpose, and how to put it into practice. I grew up in a saved household; in fact, I am a preacher's kid. I am the daughter of a bishop and a prophetess, and they are both pastor churches. Growing up, I often heard my mother praying in her room. She would talk to God for two or three hours at a time (something I still can't do), but her prayers were and are answered, and usually there is some great testimony that follows. When I got saved, I shouted, I danced, I spoke in tongues, but I did not pray consistently. Every Wednesday night and Sunday morning, I made my way to the altar for someone else to pray for me. I got my fix, and immediately I would leave the altar feeling refreshed, empowered, and renewed—that was until some new problem or situation arose and my fix wore off.

You see, because I was not seeking God for myself, I did not know how to weather the storms of life, and I was living off the prayers of others. I could not understand why I was not growing and why my walk with Christ was so up, down, and devoid of any real power. It wasn't until I started praying that I started seeing God move mightily in my life. It wasn't until I started praying that God begin to talk to me and sharing His will me. My hope is that as you spend time reading this chapter, God will open the eyes of our understanding concerning our need to pray.

With all of the media coverage surrounding the violent acts that have taken place over the past few months, and even more so in the last few days, there has been an increased call to corporate prayer as never seen before. People from every nationality, color, creed, religious affiliation, and socio-economic background are being asked to come together to pray for each other, this nation, and the world as a whole. In addition, as children of God, we encounter people who will request the all too familiar, "Pray for me." When we acknowledge difficulties in another's life, we will offer up the well-meaning cliché, "I'll be praying for you." Often times, I wonder if we really know what we are saying and agreeing to when we tell a person that we will be praying for them. Are we being sincere when we utter those all too familiar words? Or has the practice of saying them become so common-place and cliché? We often go about our daily routines, never giving thought to the promise we have made and never talking to God on behalf of that individual.

Allow me to be transparent for a moment. I can honestly say in times past I have uttered those same words to people, and while I meant well, I never spoke an intercessory word on behalf of that person and his or her situation. And if we were all to be very transparent, we have all done this and have offered a half-hearted, "Lord, bless them" in passing. May God forgive us for not honoring our word to intercede for those individuals. With our society in the shape it is in right now—the violence, broken homes, disobedient children, homosexuality, and promiscuity prevailing in the land—there is no time like the present in which we should do as 2 Chronicles 7:14 (KJV) says, and that is to "humble ourselves and pray!" Not a clichéd response to what is going on around us, but a prayer that seeks God's will and direction for our lives and the lives of others.

Although we mean well, we must stop giving people popular clichés to make them feel better about their situation; we must truly pray for them. But the sad part about prayer is that although it is a tool for spiritual warfare at our disposal, it is often under-utilized, neglected, misunderstood, and forfeited by the people of God. Sadly, God's people don't always make it a priority. A phenomenon that I have been studying and reading about, and one that is plaguing churches across the land, is the fact that many of its members do not pray. If they do, they do not pray consistently.

People will show up in droves to hear the preacher preach a word; they will come and listen to singing, and they will be in attendance to hear a word of prophecy, but when the doors are open for prayer, there are very few members that attend regularly. Prayer seems to no longer be a priority in the lives of individual families or church-members. In addition, even in the lives of the believer, prayer is often the last resort. We will seek counsel from our friends, our family, a counselor, or even a self-help book, only turning to God when those individuals are unavailable or the advice given or found does not lead us to the solution we are seeking. Now don't get me wrong, I am not saying that we are not to seek the advice of spiritual leaders or mentors, but that they should not be a substitute for seeking God's guidance. Food for thought: the created being does not know more than the Creator. So, it only makes sense that we should go to God in prayer first.

What has happened is that instead of our prayers being a proactive stance in warfare, it has become almost completely reactionary in nature against the external and internal stimuli that we are presently facing. The external stimuli are everything going on around us in our lives that tends to rob us of our peace and rob us of our joy. The internal stimulus is our "inner-me," which has brought us thoughts of condemnation, shame, fear, and rejection. And if we don't bring those thoughts under subjection to the power and authority of Jesus

Christ, our inner-me becomes our enemy. We need to make prayer a habitual practice, not out of traditionalism, but one out of necessity. When we fail to seek God first, we prolong our suffering and our solution. And when we finally seek Him, it is as if we have said, "I might as well pray now, because nothing else I do seems to be working anyway." The caution with this practice is that we are trying to live out our lives devoid of the Father's presence—we want His presents, gift, talents, and blessings. We want those things that He can give, but we do not want Him interfering in our lives on a consistent basis. We are essentially trying to be for ourselves that which only Christ is intended to be for us, and that is our strength. When we operate in this mindset, "we have[ing] a form of godliness, but deny[ing] the power thereof..." (2 Timothy 3:5, KJV).

In order to understand why prayer is so important to our Christian walk, we must first understand what prayer is. By definition, prayer is approaching God in order to ask Him to accomplish His will on the earth (Luke 11:2-4, KJV). Prayer is our opportunity to pray out God's plan on the earth. And in order for God to perfect His will in the earth, He needs earthly participants. Further clarity can be found in Genesis 1:26. It reads:

> And God said, Let us make man in our image, after our likeness: and let them have dominion over the fish of the sea, and over the fowl of the air, and over the cattle, and over all the earth, and over every creeping thing that creepeth upon the earth.
>
> —Genesis 1:26, KJV

Because God gave authority over all the earth to mankind when He said, "let them," He legally bound Himself to His Word. Notice, God did not say "Let us" but "let them," as it pertained to dominion over the earth. By doing so, God did not include Himself as the legal authority over the earth.

Any legal assistance from Him or an angelic being dispatched on your behalf from Him from heaven is only legal through the prayers and petitions of mankind. This Scripture helps to answer the questions that I hear from so many people: "If God is so loving, why is there so much evil in the word? Why do bad things happen?" Well first, we know that earth is, and has been, in an altered state since the fall of Adam and Eve. The earth we inhabit today is not God's original design. Second, simply put, sin runs rampant on the earth because people are not praying—although they have the power and the authority to seek God on behalf of the earth.

You see, God must obtain agreement and cooperation from a person for whatever He wants to accomplish on the earth, which takes us back to 2 Chronicles 7:14. If we humble ourselves and pray, and seek his face and turn from our wicked ways (2 Chronicles 7:14, KJV). Notice the word "if" at the beginning of the scripture text. The word "If" is a conditional word, and it means everything that comes after the word "ways" in the confines of this scripture is predicated on a CONDITIONAL action. In order for us to see the forgiving of sins and the healing of our land, there are some prerequisites that are to be subscribed to. And an example of prerequisites in our daily lives is when we are in high school or in college. In order for us to take a particular class, we must have taken and fulfilled the requirements of a particular course first. If we have not completed the necessary requirements, then we cannot take the course.

So essentially what God is saying to us is if we want to see these things manifest in our lives and in the earth, we must do some things first. There must be some humbling, praying, seeking, and turning! When we pray consistently, we learn the heart of God and His will for the earth. We have to remember, "God is not a man, that He should lie; neither the son of man, that He should repent: Hath He said, and shall He not do it? Or hath He spoken, and shall he not make it good?" (Numbers 23:19, KJV). Because God bound Himself to His word and He operates out of integrity, He will not violate the law of His word. Our God is such a gentleman that He waits for us to pray to Him so that He can interfere in Earth's affairs. When we neglect to pray, we leave our lives, the lives of those we love, and the earth open to the enemy's devices.

Now don't get me wrong, even if we fail to pray, God will still accomplish His will and purpose on the earth. The only difference is that He will do it without us—He will use someone else to fulfill His purpose, and we will not have fulfilled our role in His purpose. I don't know about you, but just as Jesus reprimanded the Pharisees in Luke 19:40 (KJV) because they didn't want to see the people give Jesus praise during His triumphant entry, I don't want God to have to reprimand me for not doing what He has purposed me to do. Jesus told them, "...if these should hold their peace, the stones would immediately cry out" (Luke 19:40, KJV). And just as we shouldn't want a stone to cry out for us in praise of our Lord and Savior Jesus Christ, we shouldn't want someone else to fulfill our role as it pertains to ushering in God's assistance for kingdom work. You see, not everyone is called to be a pastor, prophet, missionary, or deacon, but everyone is called to pray. It's time to pray, saints. We also have to remember that our fight is not with flesh and blood, and because our fight is not with Man, we must use the very weapon of prayer to defeat and thwart the attacks of the enemy.

Ephesians 6:18 (KJV) says that we should be "praying always with all prayers and supplication in the spirit." Our best battle stance is one that is positioned on the knees of our heart, laying out our supplications and petitions before an Almighty God. When we spend quality time with God in communion with Him, He begins to transform our heart. Biblically, our heart is more than just the seat of our emotions and affections. It is also the place of our intellect and will. God begins to change us, and as we become more like Christ, our prayers begin to shift. We find ourselves praying out to the very will of God for our lives, the lives of our family, and for the nation as a whole. You will find that the more you pray, the longer your prayers become. And you will also find that the substance of your prayer begins to change as well. You will find yourself talking less about yourself and more about others. The Holy Ghost will often come in and help guide your prayers. You will find yourself crying less from the abundance of your pain and more from the abundance of your worship. If you want to experience God in a supernatural way, pray. If you want guidance on what your next move should be, pray. Are our kids acting up? Pray. Do you want to see your spouse become saved? Pray. Do you want to see change in our government and in the nation? Pray.

There are a few nuggets from Dr. Charles F. Stanley's book, *30 Life Principles*, I want you to think about as it concerns prayer:

1. Listening to God is essential for walking with God. In order to hear Him, we must commune with Him daily. Doing so daily will help us to determine His voice, even in the midst of chaos.[vii]

2. Adversity is a bridge to a deeper relationship with God. Why? Because adversity will often drive us to our knees. God will often use bad and/or uncomfortable situations to get our attention.[viii]

3. Disappointments are inevitable. If you live, you will have some disappointments; however, discouragement is a choice. You can choose to encourage yourself or choose to wallow in self-pity. Going to God in prayer when disappointments come will help you to retain your joy and your praise to Him will confuse the enemy.[ix]

Pray this with me: dear Lord, I repent of the times that I treated talking to You as if they were the last things I would rather do. I realize I am no good on my own. I need Your guidance so I can operate in my gifting and callings as You have purposed me from before the beginning of time. I need You now, and I believe that You hear me when I pray. I commit all of me to You for You to perfect Your perfect will in me. In Jesus' name, Amen.

CHAPTER 14
The Power of Your Voice

Thou are snared with the words of thy mouth; thou are taken with the words of thy mouth.

—Proverbs 6:2, KJV

As people, God has equipped us all with the ability to articulate our thoughts, desires, and emotions through our words. No other life-form, whether in the land, air, or sea, has the ability to do so. God's decision to make us in His image and His likeness allows us to operate in this way. Our words, when spoke truthfully and authentically from the core of who we are, convey the intentions of our hearts. Additionally, the words we speak will set the tone for how we will live our day, and ultimately, our lives. Proverbs 21:23 (AMP) teaches "He who guards his mouth and his tongue, guards his soul from troubles." When we make a conscious choice to "watch" and control what comes out of our mouths, our lives will be better for doing so.

As Christians, it is ever so important that we are careful with the words we put into the atmosphere. The words spoken can and will attach themselves to our lives, and if they are the wrong words (meaning they don't line up to God's Word), and if revelation is not given concerning them, those words have the ability to attach themselves to our lives for a lifetime. This is often where generational curses from. An ancestor may have uttered words of death in a fit of frustration, which then attached themselves to the lineage of that individual for many generations. So not only will a word affect us in the now, but those same words can affect our future and our children's future.

One day I was shopping at Walmart, and by nature (and God's design), I have a high level of awareness about people, things, and my surroundings. I don't miss much. On this day, there was a mother shopping with her three young children, and as little children are, they were very animated and rambunctious. I took note of the mother's growing frustration with her children; she could not get them to settle down long enough to get her shopping completed. She began to curse at the children and say some really awful things to them. As I listened, the Lord instructed me to go speak with her about the tone of her voice and what she was saying to her children. I can honestly say I hesitated for a minute and my thought was, "You want me to do what??!!" I really thought if I would speak to her about how she was dealing with HER children, that out of her frustration and her desire for me to mind my own business, she would curse me out too! Nevertheless, I walked over to her and commented on how cute her children were and asked her if I could share something with her. She allowed me to, and I shared with her how her words as a mother could shape her children for the good and the bad. I mentioned how negative words influence children for a lifetime. I told her that I did not believe that she would set out to intentionally harm her children; however, the things that she was saying to them had the potential to attach to her children's hearts for a lifetime, and that it would take the power of a living God to undue the harm. She became teary eyed, and I could tell that my words were resonating with her heart. She thanked me for taking out the time to talk with her, and she said that she was going to be mindful about how she dealt with and talked to her children from now on.

I wrote all of that to say this: We often don't know the full impact and weight of our statements. And in the case of this mother, she uttered some really harsh things to her children out of frustration, not meaning to harm them. However, whether intentionally or unintentionally spoken, our words have the power to heal and to hurt.

We should be careful to never throw out words idly or dismissively, because there is a lot at stake in what we say. Again, as stated before, the Bible teaches us in Proverbs 18:21 (KJV) that "Death and life are in the power of the tongue: and they that love it shall eat the fruit thereof." Essentially what this scripture is telling us is what we say has consequences. Our tongue has the ability to kill, and by that I mean it has the power to destroy lives, marriages, friendships, and churches. Ill-spoken words have the power to wage physical and mental wars, as well as annihilate a person's character. And once spoken, these words can never be taken back. We must be mindful to talk to God every day, not only to make petitions of Him, but to also repent of anything done and said so that we can break the ties that have us bound to the negative words that have been spoken. You see, often what is killing us is not what others have said and done, but what we have said and done to ourselves.

There are three aspects to consider concerning the words we speak out of our mouths, and these three aspects will often tell us where we are (and others) relationally with God.

1. Our words often challenge the authority of God's words and assert a power and thought paradigm of self-sufficiency, self-rule, and self-governance. Ex: "I will never let that happen again; I can handle everything on my own" or "I will figure it out on my own; I don't need to talk to God about it."

   John 15:5 (KJV) says, "I am the vine, ye are the branches: He that abideth in me, and I in him, the same bringeth forth much fruit: for without me ye can do nothing." This scripture reminds us when we operate out of a self-governance mindset, we are yielding to the pride of life and the enemy's deception. If it had not been for God, we could not do anything. Everything we are and everything we hope to be is tied to our covenant relationship with God the Father and the redemptive work His Son, Jesus Christ, did on the cross for us. Our rising up and our going down, as well as our talents and our gifts, come from God. Every good and perfect gift comes from God, and knowing this truth will remind us to not take credit for God's design nor think that we can do anything of in and of our own strength. We can rest assured knowing that God is our strength when we are weak. If we learn to hold onto Him, He will bear our burdens for us.

2. Our words often portray the worship and presence of idols in our lives—those idols can be people and/or things. Ex: "I have to have his or her approval before I can accept what God has told me to do" or "Once I get that promotion/house/care (etc.), I will be okay."

When we say these things, and move in the direction of acquiring them, we find ourselves in direct conflict with what the Word says. I can honestly say that I have uttered those same statement and moved in the direction of acquiring them—but God! I am thankful that God began to purge my heart and mind of the words and thought processes that were keeping me from finding my identity and purpose in Him. Exodus 20:1-3 teaches us that idol worship displeases God. It says, "And God spoke all these words saying, 'I am the Lord thy God, which brought thee out of the Land of Egypt, out of the house of bondage. Thou shalt have no other gods before me'" (Exodus 20:1-3, KJV). For the people of today, Egypt represents bondage—anything and everything that tries to control us through manipulation, fear, and idol worship. We must take control of the words that will bind us to things and people and attempt to push our hearts away from God. Remember, when God sent His Son, Jesus, He freed us from the bondage of death and gave us life more abundantly. And with this new life comes freedom if we yield to God's sovereignty in our lives.

Then and only then will we be people who are walking in the favor of God.

3. Our words often betray the purpose and will of God that has been planned for our lives. Ex: The statement, "What comes up, comes out!" is indicative of the inability to control one's mouth and is in direct conflict to the Word of God.

   Again, Proverbs 21:23 teaches us to guard our mouth and our tongue. In other words, everything that comes to your mind to say should not always be said. We need to discern whether our words will harm or heal—build or tear down. Additionally, guarding our mouth and tongue will keep us from engaging in conversations that we shouldn't be involved in. It will also keep us from the drama that is plaguing the lives of so many people. Essentially, we are to actively engage in tempering and managing the words that come out of our mouths. When a Christian says, "What comes up, comes out," it shows they lack maturity and self-control. Mathew 7:20 (KJV) teaches us, "Wherefore by their fruits ye shall know them." What a person does and says is a strong indicator of where they are relationally with God and what spirit is dominating or operating in their lives. Another statement that shows our lack of self-control is, "I cannot live without (insert the things you feel as though you cannot do without)." In what you say you cannot do without, you are saying that the God who created the Universe and everything in it is not able to free you from your fleshly desires and/or wrong thinking.

One of my favorite scriptures, 2 Corinthians 3:17 (KJV), explains it this way, "Now the Lord is that spirit: and where the spirit of the Lord is, there is Liberty." When we are of Christ, and because

He lives on the inside of us, He has freed us from being controlled by our emotions. When we are willing to submit to the sovereignty of God, He frees us from our will and our feelings. Another one of my favorite scriptures, Jeremiah 29:11, tells us that God has a plan for us that what was in place even before we were created. It says, "For I know the thoughts I think toward you, saith the Lord, thoughts of peace, and not of evil to give you an expected end" (Jeremiah 29:11, KJV). Our words must speak the plans that God has ordained for our lives. We must ask God to teach us how to hide His words in our hearts that we may not sin against Him (Psalm 119:11, KJV), but also so that we can pray and speak His words over our lives.

And just as negative words have the power to change things, so do the right words. Right words have the power to bring forth life. In fact, Proverbs 15:4 (KJV) says in the A-clause that "a wholesome tongue is the tree of life." And as we imagine a tree, we know that its roots run deep into the ground allowing it to stay steady and strong in the midst of the storm and the rain. It allows the tree to be nurtured and produce much fruit. And so it is with the right words spoken at just the right time. Proverbs 16:24 (KJV) says, "Pleasant words are as a honeycomb, sweet to the soul, and health to the bones." Another illustration of the affect good words has on the soul of man is Proverbs 12:25. It says, "Anxiety in a man's heart, weighs it down, but a good [encouraging] word makes it glad" (Proverbs 12:25, AMP). You see, the words that come out of our mouths should be edifying and should administer grace to the hearers. Ephesians 4:29 (AMP) teaches us, "Do not let unwholesome [foul, profane, worthless, vulgar] words ever come out of your mouth, but only such speech as is good for building up others, according to the need and the occasion, so that it will be a blessing to those who hear [you speak]." As you can see, OUR words have the ability to bring hope to the hopeless and understanding and light to dark, difficult situations. They have the capacity to heal broken marriages, build strong familial ties, and strengthen churches. They have the power to reconcile people and make peace.

Again, as stated before, we will know them by the fruit that they bear. And may I suggest that you will also know a person's spiritual diet by what comes out of their mouth? Why? Because what primarily comes out of your mouth depends on what is in your heart. And what is in your heart depends on what you are ingesting—what you are taking in with your eye and ear gates. Essentially, it is what you are looking at and what you are hearing. If you are overloading your senses with things that are not of God, then you will begin to exhibit characteristics and mannerisms that are not of God. Remember, our mouth is connected to our heart. If you are not taking the Word of God and making application of it on a daily basis, the Word of God is not being allowed to penetrate nor hide in your heart, and your character will not have the ability to change. Your heart remains stony and is not soft and pliable to the things of God. To bring further clarity, Luke 6:45 (KJV) teaches us that "...of the abundance of the heart, the mouth speaks." Often, if you want to know what is truly in a man or woman's heart, just disagree with them and have an argument. Often, what is said in the "heat of the moment" is the pure, unadulterated truth.

If a person has a bitter heart, you will find they often speak very harshly to others—even to those whom they say they love. Their words tend to cut and cause others to hurt, and I learned that often what they need is to find forgiveness of a past hurt because it has caused bitterness to take root in their heart. A critical heart causes us to speak words that are critical and fault-finding, and it does nothing to bring about peace or unity in a situation. When a person has an ungrateful heart, it will cause them to mumble and complain and not be able to show appreciation for the things others have done for them—including God. Individuals who have a self-righteous heart can never see the faults in themselves but carry judgmental thoughts and speech towards other people. They tend blame everyone else for their shortcoming. So, as you can see, when we communicate with hearts that have not been healed and/or been delivered, we will communicate negative words and infuse our environment with words that are in direct opposition to what God has already said about you.

In contrast, a heart that has been delivered and healed speaks positive words, and those words have the power to bring forth comfort, peace, and life. A heart that is rooted in love tends to speak words that are forgiving and kind. A heart that is faithful speaks words that are truthful and have the power to build. A heart that is full of peace speaks words of reconciliation and unification. Again, you will live out your days according to the words that come out of your mouth, and that is why it is so important that we fill our hearts with the Word of God. Our words, infused with the power of God's words, have the power to change our circumstances and breathe life into seemingly dead situations, but only when we speak according to Scripture and learn to change our vocabulary.

In biblical context, the heart is not merely the seat of our emotions and our affections, but it is the intellect and will of a person. Romans 10:8-10 says,

> But what saith it? The word is nigh thee, even in thy mouth, and in thy heart: that is the word of faith, when we preach; That if thou shalt confess with thy mouth the Lord Jesus, and shalt believe in thine heart that God hath raised him from the dead, thou shalt be saved. For with the heart man believeth unto righteousness; and with the mouth confession is made unto salvation.
>
> —Romans 10:8-10, KJV

So, in order to have all there is to have and be all there is to be through Jesus, we must SPEAK a word over our lives, but not just any word. It must be a word that is rooted and grounded in the sufficiency of God's Word.

In order to truly understand how your voice has power, we will look at a very familiar passage of scripture. Mark 11:23 teaches us the power of faith when it is connected to your voice. It says, "For verily

I say unto you, that whosoever shall say unto this mountain, Be thou removed, and be thou cast into the sea; and shall not doubt in his heart, but shall believe those things which he saith shall come to pass; he shall have whatsoever he saith" (Mark 11:23, KJV). In this parable, Jesus teaches His disciples the power of faith is VOICE activated. Many Christians have read these verses and have used a literal translation and application. They surmise that they should be able to walk over to a literal mountain of stone and it will move when they tell it to because of their faith. However, that is not rally what the scripture means. In an effort to understand this text of scripture, we must be able to recognize that Jesus often taught His disciples using parables.

A parable is a simple story used to illustrate a moral or spiritual lesson, as told by Jesus in the gospels. In this parable, Jesus shows us how this voice principle works with our faith. If you notice in the text, the mountain will not move until it is spoken to. The mountain is representative of the issues in your life. And if you do not speak to those problems, the problems will not move. Notice, Jesus did not tell you to speak to your neighbor's mountain, He told you to speak to YOUR mountain. The issues in your life are yours, and they must obey your voice. You must use your tongue to speak to your own mountain if you want to see it move. And in order to see the mountain move, our voice must be in agreement with God's will and His plan. How will we know God's plan? God reveals His plan through the reading of His word and through our fasting and praying.

You see, we can't just name it and claim it, because many things we are naming and claiming are not in God's will for our lives. Either our voice will open the way or be in the way. When we put the Word of God in our hearts, our voices will speak the character and plan of God. Our words, in partnership with God's plan, will cause our souls to be saved, husbands to come back home, and wayward children to become obedient. Speaking a positive word coupled with putting our faith in action will cause us to walk in the favor of God. It will cause us to have a "Yes, Lord" in our spirit, and we can walk with spiritual boldness decreeing and declaring God's words over our lives and others. No longer are we to sit back and allow the enemy to wreak havoc in our lives. We can SPEAK a word to the enemy and serve him notice that our words and our lives will advance the kingdom of God. We will no longer be silent but will declare the works of the Lord. Remember: when we are silent, we lose by default!

Declaration Time: Lord, I repent of any idle word spoken from my mouth that does not agree with Your plan and will for my life. I decree and declare that my words will bring healing, reconciliation, peace, and comfort. I will speak to those issues in my life and declare only what You say about them. I will not shut down, and I will not give up! I will use my voice in partnership with my faith in You to bring about a positive change in my life!

Barbara Steger

CHAPTER 15

Bonus Chapter from My Sermon, "Letting Go and Letting God"

"God is our refuge and strength, a very present help in trouble."

—Psalm 46:1, NKJV

As I prepared for this event, I found myself becoming restless because God had not yet deposited in my spirit what He wanted me to convey. I started praying more in preparation and even reading more because I was sure the Lord was going to speak well in advance of this date, and I would have my speaking points ready and have an outline of what I was going to say. However, that was far from the truth. I would toss and turn at night the week leading up to the event, and I still had not heard Him speak.

It wasn't until Wednesday of that week I began to get an inkling of what God wanted to express through me. And as I thought of the theme of the conference, I really wasn't sure how to approach it. I even struggled for many weeks with how to articulate what the heart of the theme truly meant. It wasn't until the Wednesday prior I understood the difficulty. Letting go and letting God isn't as easy as people make it out to be. That saying has become a cliché for many; it has become the go-to phrase for when we have difficulty, and we cannot seem to see our way through.

You see, when you are going through difficult times and situations, it is very hard to focus on the good in that situation. It is often hard for us to grasp that God sees our struggles, hears our cries, or that He even knows when we pray. I don't know about you, but at times it seems as if my prayers only go as high as the ceiling, never reaching the ears of God. For years, I thought that I had to feel something when I prayed, and I believed that the feeling would be an indication that God had heard my petition. You see, as a woman, by God's design we are emotional beings. And because we are, we must be mindful not to approach prayer from an emotional standpoint. Why? Because God is not attracted to your problems, He is attracted to your praise!

And so over the course of my walk with Christ, I heard the patriarchs in the church say, "Let Go and let God have His way." And I would always question in my heart, "How do I do that?" How do I do that when there are more bills than there is money? How do I let go and let God when my marriage is falling apart? My children are acting up? The boss on my job seems to hate me? So, I often questioned God by asking, "God, is this your plan?" Seriously? If we are to be honest, we have all questioned God at some point, and we have wondered "Where is He in all of this mess?" Because the Bible teaches us in 1 Corinthians 14:33 (KJV) that "God is not the author of confusion," right? That was my very dismal human attempt to explain away my inability to understand God's sovereign plan and purpose for my life and the lives of those I love. It wasn't until I became more seasoned in the Word of God that I could truly understand the meaning of this verse in the context of how God moves or allows things to happen in our lives.

The scripture that God gave me to better understand the theme of Letting Go and Letting is from 2 Samuel, and it reads,

> Again David gathered all the choice men of Israel, thirty thousand. And David arose and went with all the people who were with him from Baale Judah to bring up from the ark of God, whose name is called by the Name, the Lord of Hosts, who dwells between the cherubim. So they set the ark of God on a new cart,

and brought it out of the house of Abinidab, which was on the hill; and Uzzah and Ahio, the sons of Abinidab, drove the new cart. And they brought it out of the house of Abinidab, which was on the hill, accompanying the ark of God; and Ahio went before the ark. Then David and all the house of Israel played music before the Lord on all kinds of instruments of fir wood, on harps, on stringed instruments, on tambourines, on sistrums, and on cymbals. And when they came to Nachon's threshing floor, Uzzah put out his hand to the ark of God and took hold of it, for the oxen stumbled. Then the anger of the Lord was aroused against Uzzah, and God struck him there for His error, and he died there by the ark of God. And David became angry because of the Lord's outbreak with Uzzah and he called the name of the place Perez Uzzah to this day.

—2 Samuel:1-8, KJV

Now, one might ask the question, "How do these verses tie into the title's chapter, 'Letting Go and Letting God?'" Just to give you a little background, the Ark of the Covenant had been taken by the Philistines a generation earlier when David defeated the Philistines and eventually got the Ark back. The Arc symbolized God's relationship with His people. It normally remained in the most holy place, and His presence would appear above it–making it one of the most sacred articles of Israel's worship. What David did was foolish and immature. David failed to consult the Word of God before he moved the Ark; if he had done so prior to moving it, he would have learned the specific way the Lord instructed His people to transport it. God never blesses any violation of His will.

So again, how does this story and these verses tie into the theme that was selected for the women's conference? The revelation that God gave to me is this: we often try holding onto things that He did not tell us to hold on to or that He alone is responsible for the safe keeping of. David had not consulted the Lord as to how the Ark was to be carried, and because of this error in judgement it cost a man his life.

Well, when we think about all the hats we tend to wear as women and the endless duties that come with those roles and responsibilities, we know that there is more to do than there are hours in the day. We are being pulled in a million different directions. We are responsible for the upkeep of our homes, the nurturing of our children. We are working outside of the home and have responsibilities in the church. We are busy, and because everyone seems to depend on us, we often feel it is our responsibility to fix everything—in our own strength and without consulting God first. We are trying to be the glue that holds everything together, and yet, we are dying spiritually, emotionally, and even physically. The stress of life is catching up to us and we are walking around with high blood pressure and having headaches, and we are just sick and tired—but mostly tired.

We have gotten so busy with the cares of this life that we forget to make time to talk to God, as David had been. He was too busy celebrating the retrieval of the Ark that he forgot to consult God about how the Ark was to be handled. We get so busy with our lives that we forget to consult God on how He wishes to handle us. In order to be the very embodiment of God's will, we must be careful to consult God in every season of our lives. When we fail to do so, we will find that we are often holding on to things that the Lord is trying to take from us. Or we are carrying things and people that He never intended for us to carry. And while we may not experience a sudden death like Uzzah, we will eventually feel our spiritual man become weaker and weaker because we have not accepted the totality of God's purpose and plan for our lives.

You see, trusting the process by which God moves or allows things to happen in our lives is just as important as the plan. We can't have faith in His plan and then despise the process. It should be the desire of every Christian woman and man to be the very embodiment of God's will. It is not enough to desire to be in the center of His will. We must want to the be embodiment—the actual walking, talking, and breathing example of who God is and what He can do when our will is completely surrendered to Him. And we do this by consulting God consistently in every season of our lives. When we fail to do so, we will find that we are often holding on to things that the Lord is trying to take from us or we are carrying people and things He did not intend for us to carry. Often, God is trying to take us to higher heights and deeper depths and position you for your next level, but because we don't have the spiritual sense to let go, we become spiritual sons and daughters that live beneath our privilege as a children of the Most High. And then we become people of God who are powerless, not because God has no power, but because we won't open our moth to cry out to God to ask Him for spiritual wisdom, strength, and guidance.

We are doing a whole lot of crying out to others, but not talking to God. Remember, life and death lie in the power of YOUR tongue, and you lose by default if you do not speak to the situation from a kingdom mind-set. We have not put our faith in the very nature (character) of God. We have a form of godliness, but we deny the power that comes from God. What must be understood is that trusting the process by which God moves is just as important as His plan. For it is in the enduring, persevering, and obeying that will bring forth the blessing of the Lord. Having faith in His plan means we are to trust that God's timing and the way in which He moves on our behalf is what is best for us. We cannot have faith in His plan and then despise the process by which His plan unfolds. I can honestly say that I am like many of you—understanding and trusting God's process has been a lifelong struggle of mine.

For years I carried around the shame and condemnation of being molested as a child and raped when I was sixteen. I could not understand why God, in His infinite wisdom, would allow such a thing to happen to me. Although I grew up in a Christian household, and heard the testimonies about how good God is, because of my pain,

I rebelled against the knowledge of Christ. I thought, if He is so great and loving, He would not have allowed those things to happen to me. On many occasions over the course of my life, various people prophesized that I had a prophetic all on my life—that I would somehow be God's mouthpiece. But because of the hurt from those earlier events in my life, I could not see why God would want to use somebody like me, a skinny little black girl with tattoos and a nose ring from Nowhere, USA. And so, because I could not identify with God's Word spoken over my life, I rebelled. One day, God really got a hold of me, and I got tired of running from Him and the prophetic mantle on my life. I mustered up enough courage to ask, "Why me?" And God answered. It was not some loud thunderous boom from heaven's gates. It was a still small voice that answered with a question, "Why not you?"

He then began to share with me that those events in my life happened so that others could be helped. You see, I was to help others that experienced the same pain, the same shame, and heartache. It would make me relatable to some other young woman or young man because I, too, had gone through the same thing. I could share God's love and resurrected power because He had changed me and made me new. He used those events to mold me and shape me to bring me to a place in Him that I could finally understand my identity. Those events weren't about the past me, they were about the future me. The me that I could not see. God's process in bringing me to a place of self-awareness was nothing I would have chosen for myself, but because He is sovereign, I learned to accept the purpose in my pain. And what we have to remember is that God loves us too much to waste our pain. As Romans 8:28 (KJV) tells us, "And we know that all things work together for good to them that love God, to them who are the called according to His purpose." EVERYTHING that we experience in our lives—good and bad, happy or sad, disappointments, set-backs and set-ups, and even death—it all has a divine purpose in the life of a believer. God will often use the worst situation to bring you to a place in Him. You see, as tragic as Uzzuh's death was, it could have been prevented. Through the process of Uzzuh's death, King David, anointed and appointed by God—and a man after God's own heart—learned a valuable lesson. He learned that he needed to inquire of the Lord before making a decision for God's people, because if he did not, others would suffer as the result of his failure to hear from God. The overarching question is can we let go and let God? Can we have faith in His plan and His purpose for our lives? Can we trust Him even when we don't get the outcome that we want for ourselves? The Bible teaches us in Proverbs 19:21 (NIV) that "many are the plans in a man's heart, but it's the Lord's will that prevails." Make no assumptions or mistakes about it—God's will will prevail, and we don't always need or get what we think is right for ourselves. The sooner we understand the truth of that scripture, the better we can walk in the favor of God and begin to grow stronger in Him walking in victory and power. We will be able to decree and declare some things over our lives. We can boldly say that we will live and not die and declare the works of the Lord!

Another takeaway from this passage of Scripture is that we can be cruising along in life and think we are heading in the right direction We will make plans to follow our personal dreams and aspirations, but because we have not consulted God in the matter, we may find ourselves out of the will of God. Due to our disobedience, chastisement and conviction comes, and so does the consequence. You see, King David was in the midst of celebrating having beaten the Philistines, and now he, a newly appointed king, had positioned himself to be the one to bring the Ark of the Covenant back home to safety. Can you imagine how he must have felt? The pure joy, elation, and pride he must have felt? And so, he had his men bring the Ark back, which was a good thing; however, he did so without consulting God to see what was the proper way to handle the Ark.

We must be able to discern the difference between a good thing and a God thing. Everything that glitters isn't gold, and sometimes the enemy will bring a substitute dressed up to look real appealing to confuse you into thinking it is what God want you have. Some things we want to do or want to have aren't bad—a new car or house, a promotion on our job, getting married, or even going back to college. We would even say that those things are good things. However, the good becomes bad when we push our agenda to the forefront without consulting God in the matter. His plan for that season of our life may not involve us going back to school. The late hours at school may not be in the best interest of our family unit and may push your spouse to seek friendship in someone else's arms. The children may begin to rebel in the home and at school because there is no one home to supervise—you get the point. While not necessarily a bad thing, we must learn to consult God first so that we handle ourselves according to his plan because God will not operate outside of His will and purpose for your life, and He definitely will not bless a mess. His very nature simply won't allow Him to do so.

We have all been there. Things seem to be great for a while and then something comes out of nowhere. We wonder, "God, where are you?" And the truth of the matter is that He hasn't gone anywhere. He is always present and has been waiting for us to cry out to Him for His guidance and support. See, I don't know about you, but there have been times in my life that I mishandled me. My inner-me became my enemy. I did all kinds of things that would make a preacher blush! I let the enemy control my mind and my body. I even mishandled others because of my preconceived idea on what I believed was best for them based upon the situation they presented. There was a time that I almost failed God based on what I felt was a detriment to another person's life.

I had an incident in which I was at work one day and began to cry and could not figure out why I was so emotional. I was going to college full-time and had taken on a new role as an assistant principal. I was split between two title one elementary schools. I was overworked, over-whelmed, under-paid, and just plain tired. I thought the uncertainty and stress of the new position had finally caught up with me and was the source of my tears. I cried all day, and by the time I made the forty-minute commute home, I looked like a puffer fish. My eyes and face were swollen, and my nose was red. I looked horrible! My husband too immediately noticed and asked me what was wrong. However, I could not articulate my feelings—which was so unlike me. Words are my thing, and I have never had a problem expressing myself. All I knew was that I could not express what I was feeling, and what I was feeling literally felt like death. As if I was grieving the loss of someone very close, yet, no one had passed away. Let's fast forward a few days. A domestic violence incident transpired that caused me to find out that my unmarried daughter of twenty-two years was pregnant. My baby was going to have a baby, and I was not prepared for that! I immediately became fearful for of her future. I was angry, hurt, disappointed, and, to a great degree, embarrassed. You see, her father and I had taught her better, and getting pregnant without the benefit of marriage is not the plan WE had for her life.

I went into "Mommy-mode" and called a family meeting. In times of crisis, I turn into Olivia Pope from Scandal, and I run in to save the day. And this family crisis was no exception. My husband, Fred, and I talked to her about the pregnancy and asked her what her plans were. She stated that she had been thinking about having an abortion, and that she would return to college as she had planned. I remember thinking to myself, "Well, I am not going to tell her to do it or not to do it because it is her body. She will be the one who will have to live with her decision, not me." No sooner than the thought came, I immediately felt a deep conviction pervade my soul. It over-shadowed me like a weighted blanket, and I could hear the voice of the Lord say, "If you don't tell her what is right, who will?"

You see, my husband is not a professing Christian (yet!), and so his views on things like this differs greatly from mine. I could not go along with what was being said in that moment. So, I began to talk to her about keeping the baby and shared with her that children are a gift from God, regardless of the circumstances that brought them to the earth. I assured her that if she were to keep the child, her father and I would support her decision and help her in any way that we could. After we talked, she went to my room and stayed a while. Sensing that she may have needed to talk, I went to go check on her. She shared that she had made the decision to keep her baby, but that she was scared. I reassured her that God was in all of this (even though it didn't look like it or feel like it). Remember the "process" I told you about earlier? My daughter eventually went back to her apartment, and my husband and I went to bed. I must have slept about an hour or two before I woke up. I could hear the Lord calling out to me and the conversation went like this:

"Barbara, do you remember a few days ago when you were crying, and you didn't know why?"

And I said, "Yes Lord."

He then asked, "Do you remember how it felt?"

I answered and said, "Yes Lord, it felt like death. It was the worst feeling I have ever had."

He said, "Well here's the thing. The feeling that I allowed you to experience was the baby's spirit crying out from its mother's womb. I needed you to be sensitive in that moment so that his spirit could connect to your spirit. I allowed the baby's spirit to cry out to you from the spiritual realm and touch your spirit-man so that you would be sensitive enough to get Amber to do the right thing."

You see, this unborn child, this wonderful gift of God, knew his life was in danger and needed to be saved. God impressed upon the baby's spirit that he could touch my spirit, and by doing so, God would use me to save its life. Had I mishandled my daughter and her situation in that moment (like I almost did), my sweet grandbaby, Sebastian Nathanial Steger, would not be here today. He is four years old (going on thirty), and he helps to keep my daughter grounded.

God is using this little guy to bring order and accountability to his mother's life. And when I write and say that he is joined to his grandma's hip! He loves his grandma and thinks he is supposed to be with me all the time! We have an undeniable connection and bond—one that was created when God allowed the supernatural to supersede the natural. You see, God's plan doesn't always mirror what we think we want for ourselves or what we may want for those we love, but we must be willing to accept and embrace it. For the sake of their lives and our own, we must learn to let go and let God have His way.

After King David got over his anger and fear, he did the right thing by consulting the Lord, and he eventually was able to take the Ark of the Covenant back three months later. And the same goes for us—when we learn to consult God and relinquish any rights we feel we have in a certain situation, God will give you the plan and take you through the process, and you WILL come out victorious. Remember, "The steps of a good man are ordered by the Lord and he delighteth in his way" (Psalm 37:23, KJV).

As Christians, if we want to walk in the favor of God, we are to be reminded that we must be willing to give up anything that may be hindering our walk or holding us back. We must take our hands off stuff God did not intend for us to carry. We have to learn not to mishandle ourselves and others, and we must trust God and His process. Because when we do, God's supernatural will supersedes our natural and causes us to rest in the promises of God. We become people who know without a shadow of a doubt that letting go and letting God have His way will allow us to fulfill the destiny and purpose God ordained at the foundation of the Word for our lives.

Declaration: God, forgive me for those times in which I mishandled myself and others. Forgive me for not consulting You to see what You would have me do or say in a particular situation. I now know that if I am to walk in all that You have created me to do, I must be willing to let go and let You have Your way in my life. I refuse to walk blindly. I give You permission to guide my step, and I give myself permission to follow. I know that wherever You lead me is good for me, and I do not have to worry about ever being lost in You, because You said in Your Word that You would never leave me nor forsake me. I trust You. I trust Your plan. And I trust the process. I am walking in the favor of God! In Jesus' name, Amen!

ENDNOTES

i "Commitment," Merriam-Webster.com. Retrieved October 25, 2020, from http://www.merriam-webster.com/dictionary/commitment.

ii "Reflection," Oxford English dictionary, Retrieved October 25, 2020, from https://en.oxforddictionaries.com/definition/Reflection.

iii "Rejection," Merriam-Webster.com, Retrieved October 25, 2020, from http:// www.merriam-webster.com/dictionary /rejection.

iv "Inevitable," Oxford English dictionary, Retrieved October 25, 2020, from https://en.oxforddictionaries.com/definition/Inevitable.

v "Identity," 2020, YourDictionary, YourDictionary.com.

vi "Identity Crisis," Oxford English dictionary, Retrieved October 25, 2020, from https://en.oxforddictionaries .com/definition/Identity Crisis.

vii Dr. Charles F. Stanley, 30 Life Principles (Atlanta, Georgia: In Touch Ministries, 2008), 63.

viii Dr. Charles F. Stanley, 30 Life Principles (Atlanta, Georgia: In Touch Ministries, 2008), 132.

ix Dr. Charles F. Stanley, 30 Life Principles (Atlanta, Georgia: In Touch Ministries, 2008), 98.

AUTHOR BIO

Barbara Steger is a minister, educator, coach, wife, mother, and grandmother. She is a former Army sergeant, 10th grade English teacher, and assistant principal. She obtained a Bachelor and Master's in English Language Arts Education, as well as both a Master's and an Education Specialist Degree in Instructional Leadership and Administration. She is also a John C. Maxwell certified speaker, coach, and mentor. She is currently the Adult Education Director for Wallace Community College in Dothan, AL. Truly a woman after God's own heart, she desires to see the people of God walk in freedom, godly wisdom, and power.

Follow her on Facebook, LinkedIn, or Instagram under the username @Barbara Steger or on Twitter @b_steger. She can be reached by email at basteger1@gmail.com.

CPSIA information can be obtained
at www.ICGtesting.com
Printed in the USA
LVHW011119210121
676968LV00007B/718